CALL HIM
JACK

JACK

THE STORY OF
JACKIE ROBINSON,
BLACK FREEDOM FIGHTER

YOHURU WILLIAMS
and MICHAEL G. LONG

FARRAR STRAUS GIROUX
New York

Farrar Straus Giroux Books for Young Readers
An imprint of Macmillan Publishing Group, LLC
120 Broadway, New York, NY 10271 • mackids.com

Our books may be purchased in bulk for promotional, educational,
or business use. Please contact your local bookseller or the Macmillan
Corporate and Premium Sales Department at (800) 221-7945, ext. 5442,
or by email at MacmillanSpecialMarkets@macmillan.com.

Library of Congress Cataloging-in-Publication Data

Names: Williams, Yohuru R., author | Long, Michael G., author.
Title: Call him Jack : the story of Jackie Robinson, Black freedom fighter /
    Yohuru Williams and Michael G. Long.
Description: First edition | New York, N.Y. : Farrar Straus Giroux Books
    for Young Readers, 2022. | Includes bibliographical references and
    index. | Audience: Ages 10–14 | Audience: Grades 4–6 | Summary: "An
    enthralling, eye-opening portrayal of this barrier-breaking American
    hero as a lifelong, relentlessly proud fighter for Black justice and civil
    rights"— Provided by publisher.
Identifiers: LCCN 2022013807 | ISBN 9780374389956 (hardcover)
Subjects: LCSH: Robinson, Jackie, 1919–1972—Juvenile literature. | African
    American baseball players—Biography—Juvenile literature. | African
    Americans—Civil rights—History—20th century—Juvenile literature. |
    Civil rights movements—United States—History—20th century—Juvenile
    literature.
Classification: LCC GV865.R6 W535 2022 | DDC 796.357092 [B]—dc3/
    eng/20220625
LC record available at https://lccn.loc.gov/2022013807

First edition, 2022
Book design by The Cosmic Lion
Printed in the United States of America by Lakeside Book Company,
Harrisonburg, Virginia

ISBN 978-0-374-38995-6 (hardcover)
10 9 8 7 6 5 4 3 2 1

Frontispiece: Jack Robinson in 1949, during his time with the Brooklyn Dodgers

*To our readers
and their fight to advance
the legacy of Jack Roosevelt Robinson*

If I had to choose between baseball's Hall of Fame and first-class citizenship, I would say first-class citizenship to all my people.

—JACK ROOSEVELT ROBINSON

CONTENTS

OUR WORDS

The words we choose to describe ourselves and one another can be respectful, kind, or cruel. They can make us smile and frown, laugh and cry, and cheer and jeer. They can make friends and enemies at the same time.

In choosing words for this book, we've tried to be as respectful as possible while still presenting the challenges that Jack Robinson faced because of the color of his skin.

We use "Black American," "African American," and "Black" to describe Jack and other Black people in the United States. We also typically use "white" to describe Americans of European descent. Plus, when we use the words "Black" and "white," we employ them as adjectives rather than nouns, because skin color is just one part of our identity. It does not define everything about us.

When quoting other people's words, we've not changed or censored them. Our quotations sometimes include outdated words to describe Black people—for example, "Negro" and "colored." These words are part of our shared history, and we think it's important for readers to know about them.

Our quotations also contain hurtful words. The one that might shock or upset readers is the word "nigger." We find this word repulsive, but we think it's important for readers to know—and feel—the words that white people used when trying to hurt Jack and other Black Americans.

PART I

FOUNDATIONS

ONE

TAKING THE FREEDOM TRAIN

It was hog-butchering day, and Mallie Robinson was excited. Perhaps Jerry would bring home a slab of bacon, some juicy ham, or a tender rack of ribs. Even part of a shoulder, along with a few feet and knuckles, would be mouthwatering additions to the menu.

With squealing and gunshots in the distance, she probably thought of her husband slicing the hog fat, carving the meat, and trimming the choice cuts. Jerry was a skilled butcher and one of the best workers on the plantation.

At the end of the day, Jerry handed Mallie the rewards of his labor. Unwrapping the butcher paper, she couldn't believe what she saw—a putrid pile of hog livers and lungs.

She felt as if someone had kicked her in the stomach. "Where's the backbones?" she demanded. "Where's the neckbones?" It was one thing not to have ham or tenderloin, but no backbone to scrape a bit of meat from? No neckbone for broth? That was unacceptable.

But there was no easy solution. The Robinsons lived on a plantation owned by a cruel white man, and Black workers had few options when they didn't receive their fair share.

Mallie was livid. Directing her ire toward Jerry, she said what they both knew all too well—"Slavery's over!"

Mallie McGriff and Jerry Robinson first caught each other's attention at a Christmas-tree-trimming party in 1903. The festivity was held on James Sasser's plantation just outside Cairo, Georgia, where Jerry's family lived and labored. "I sure like you," Jerry said as they walked to her house after the party.

Mallie's father, Washington McGriff, a former enslaved person and now a farm owner, was far from pleased when he learned that his fourteen-year-old daughter had made plans to go to church with the nineteen-year-old Jerry. Mallie's mother, Edna Sims McGriff, wasn't supportive, either. She and Washington hoped that their daughter would marry the eligible bachelor who lived in the plantation's biggest house.

But Mallie was strong-willed, independent, and determined. Despite her parents' best efforts to break them apart, she and Jerry dated for six years before marrying on November 21, 1909, less than one month before that disappointing butchering day.

When the young couple moved into a log cabin on Sasser's land, Mallie turned to her husband and said, "Let's prove to the world what we can do." But that was easier said than done. As a laborer, Jerry earned just twelve dollars a month, barely enough to feed and clothe the two of them, let alone the babies who would no doubt arrive.

Mallie soon pitched to Jerry a bold plan. "Let's try and farm for ourselves," she said. Jerry was hesitant, but sometime after the couple's first Christmas together, he approached Sasser and threatened to leave unless he could "half-crop"—farm the land and keep half the crops that he and Mallie raised.

Sasser realized that losing an excellent worker would deliver a financial blow, so he reluctantly allowed the Robinsons to start their own farming venture. Within a few years, the hardworking couple had a yard full of hogs, chickens, and turkeys, and fields with cotton, corn, peanuts, peas, beans, and potatoes.

The remains of Jack's birthplace in Grady County, Georgia

Still, not everything was good at the Robinson home. Jerry was attracted to other women, and he often left Mallie to fend for herself. By the eighth year of their marriage, the couple had separated and reconciled more than a few times. "And every time we got back together, I got another child," Mallie recalled.

She became pregnant again in the spring of 1919. The Robinsons already had four rambunctious children—Edgar, Frank, Mack, and Willa Mae—and Mallie hoped for a girl to add some balance to the brood.

She went into labor on January 31, 1919. The visiting doctor wanted to administer a painkiller, but Mallie feared that it would kill her, so she just gritted her teeth and pushed hard until he arrived—Jack Roosevelt Robinson. She named her newborn son after former president Theodore Roosevelt, who had died earlier that month.

PRESIDENT THEODORE ROOSEVELT

In 1901, President Roosevelt invited Booker T. Washington for dinner at the White House. Washington was the founder of the Tuskegee Normal and Industrial Institute in Tuskegee, Alabama. The all-Black school reflected Washington's belief that Black people could best advance their rights by becoming educated, working hard, and strengthening their moral character *within* the system of racial segregation.

A 1903 lithograph of Booker T. Washington and President Roosevelt at the White House

The dinner marked the first time that a Black man dined at the White House with a sitting US president. An uproar followed. Washington became the target of death threats, and Roosevelt endured vicious criticism from racist politicians. But Black people across the country, including Mallie Robinson, admired Roosevelt, and many considered him a supporter of Black interests. Roosevelt continued to consult with Washington, but he never again invited a Black leader to the White House.

In 1906, Roosevelt shared his secret feelings about Black people in a letter to a friend. "As a race and in the mass they are altogether inferior to the whites," he wrote. In 1916, he also claimed that "the great majority of Negroes in the South are wholly unfit for the suffrage," the right to vote. Mallie would not have known of Roosevelt's racist thoughts when she named Jack after him.

Six months later, Jerry traveled to nearby Cairo, hopped aboard train number 230, and left for Florida with another woman. Mallie wondered whether she could manage to take care of the children, feed the animals, clean the pens, and harvest the crops.

Plantation owner James Sasser was unsympathetic. He had never liked Mallie and had even called her "about the sassiest nigger ever on this place." It wasn't long before he evicted the Robinsons from their home, forcing them to move to a dilapidated property. He soon kicked them out of that one, too, saying they had to move to a house full of men.

Mallie was so upset that she gathered her children and walked off the plantation forever, leaving behind fifteen hogs, four barrels of syrup, four bales of cotton, and basketfuls of potatoes and vegetables.

Negro's Charred Body In Ashes of Church

By Associated Press

EASTMAN, Ga., Aug. 28.—The charred body of Eli Cooper, a negro, was found in the ashes of a negro church burned by incendiaries. Three other negro churches and a negro lodge in this section were burned Tuesday night.

The acts of violence followed reports the negroes planned to "rise up and wipe out the white people," and that Cooper remarked the negroes "had been run out for 50 years, but this will all change in 30 days."

The only explanations for the burning of the churches and lodgerooms was that these were said to have been the scenes of mass meetings recently during which the uprising of negroes was discussed. Hundreds of copies of a Chicago negro newspaper were said to have been distributed at these meetings.

Cooper was taken from his home Wednesday night, according to his wife, by a crowd of about 20 white men.

This was just one of numerous assaults against Black people across the South during "the Red Summer of 1919," a frightening period of race riots and bloodshed. (Los Angeles Evening Express, August 29, 1919)

The future looked bleak. Mallie found work as a maid, but the job failed to provide her with a stable economic life.

The future also looked deadly. The Ku Klux Klan was riding through Georgia once again, and in the summer of 1919, the white terrorists had burned Black churches, lodges, schools, and homes in the state.

Mallie looked for a way to escape, but there was no clear path forward—until her brother, Burton Thomas, encouraged her to move to California, the state he had migrated to years earlier.

Feeling inspired, Mallie quickly made plans with her sister Cora and her brother Paul and their families to leave Georgia for good.

THE KU KLUX KLAN (KKK)

Klan members in Valdosta, Georgia, 1922

The Ku Klux Klan was founded in Tennessee in 1866, just after the conclusion of the Civil War. Its goals were to promote white supremacy, the belief that white people are superior to people of color, and to resist Radical Reconstruction, the federal government's plan to increase the political and economic power of former enslaved people. The Klan sought to accomplish these goals by terrorizing, torturing, and lynching Black people. The original Klan disbanded in the 1870s, though remnants remained, and a new one was founded at Stone Mountain, Georgia, in 1915, shortly after the release of *The Birth of a Nation*, a blockbuster film that glorified the first Klan.

On May 21, 1920, Mallie, sixteen-month-old Jack, and his four siblings waited for the steam engine and its passenger cars to pull into the station. Mallie called it the "Freedom Train."

After everyone was safely aboard, she could finally take a deep breath. Mallie and her children were free at last. Free from the plantation. Free from Sasser. Free from white terror. And free to create a better life. Or so she thought.

The Cairo train station from which the Robinsons left for California in May 1920

Jack, probably in 1925, about age six

TWO

THROWING STONES

The train car rocked back and forth as Mallie struggled to hold Jack still. He was a strong toddler, and it was a challenge to change his diaper in the best of circumstances. As soon as he wriggled free, Jack waddled off to join his siblings.

Whenever she could, Mallie looked out the window and enjoyed the roaring rivers, the majestic mountains, and the desert valleys. The best part of the trip was seeing the bright lights of Los Angeles in early June 1920. It was "the most beautiful sight of my whole life," she remembered.

The thirteen members of the Georgia family disembarked in Pasadena, about a dozen miles outside of Los Angeles, where Mallie's brother Burton lived. With little money among them, the new arrivals moved into a dilapidated apartment near the train station. It had three small rooms, a bathroom without a tub, and old pipes with only cold water.

The Robinsons slept in one room. As the youngest, Jack shared the bed with his mother while his siblings spread themselves across the hard floor.

The day after arriving, Mallie found domestic work that paid eight dollars a week and ended every day around 4:00 P.M., giving her time to feed and care for her children. Although that job didn't last long, she soon landed a similar one with the Dodges, a white family who employed her for the next two decades.

THE GREAT MIGRATION

Migrants arriving in Chicago in 1920

The Robinsons' move from Georgia to California was part of the Great Migration. In 1920, there were twelve million Black Americans living in the United States, 75 percent of them in the South, where slavery had been most prominent. Between 1915 and 1970, more than six million Black people migrated from the South to major cities in the Northeast, Midwest, and West, including New York City, Cleveland, Detroit, Chicago, and Los Angeles. Isabel Wilkerson, author of *The Warmth of Other Suns*, a book about the migration, said, "They left on their own accord for as many reasons as there are people who left. They made a choice that they were not going to live under the system into which they were born anymore, and in some ways, it was the first step that the nation's servant class ever took without asking."

In 1922, when Jack was about three years old, Mallie and her brother-in-law Sam Wade bought a house at 121 Pepper Street. The two adults were still rather poor, but the seller agreed to "easy terms" of payment.

The house had eleven rooms, two bathrooms, a porch, fruit trees, and a yard big enough for planting vegetables, raising chickens, and playing sports. But there was a major problem. The Robinsons and Wades were the only Black people on their street, and most neighbors did not want them living there.

> 11-ROOM HOUSE, JUST PAINTED, fine plumbing, hot and cold water; bath, 2 kitchens, garage, fruit trees, large barn. Lot 70x175. Just one block off North Fair Oaks at 121 Pepper St. $5100. Easy terms. F. O. 1041. Mr. Harrison.

This advertisement for 121 Pepper Street appeared in the Pasadena Evening Post *on March 21, 1921.*

Some neighbors were so disturbed that they tried to buy the property back. When that effort failed, they burned a cross in the home's front yard. Edgar spotted the blazing wood and extinguished the flames before they could spread to the house.

If Mallie was frightened, no one detected it. They saw a strong woman who was fiercely committed to her family's right to live at 121 Pepper Street.

The Robinson kids, of course, did not stay inside their house and yard. They zipped up and down the streets, with Edgar speedily leading the way on his bike or roller skates. Legend has it that a police officer ticketed him for skating too fast.

Disapproving neighbors frequently called the police department. One man told an officer that his wife was so afraid that she had not come out of the house since the Robinsons had arrived. When the officer shared that news, Mallie remained defiant. "I'm afraid she'll be in that house a lifetime," she said.

Mallie faced another challenge. She worked during the day, and there was no one to care for young Jack when the older kids were at school. With few good options, Mallie asked Willa Mae to take her younger brother to school and leave him in the sandbox until it was time to return home.

Jack must have been surprised to find himself in the sandbox after all the other kids went inside Grover Cleveland Elementary School, but he dug in and stayed close to the windows, where his big sister could keep an eye on him. Willa Mae's teacher allowed him to come inside on rainy days and to play with students during outside recess. Jack became quite skilled at shooting acorns at all the kids running around him.

Back at home, he loved playing with a ball that Mallie had made from socks and rags. Stick in hand, he whacked the ball all around the yard, and before long, he could hit, throw, and catch as well as the older kids. Despite his "pigeon toes"—his toes pointed inward, toward each other—he also ran fast.

When Jack became a student at Cleveland Elementary, his friends stood in awe as they watched him tear up the baseball diamond, the football field, and the dodgeball court. Envious of his athletic skills, they offered him half their lunches if he would play on their side.

But his athleticism did little to protect him from the racist neighbors, and at the age of eight, he had a nasty encounter while he was sweeping the sidewalk.

Across the street was a white girl who was also sweeping. Her father was one of those who had loudly demanded that the Robinsons leave the neighborhood. Jack paid her no mind at first, but then she shouted, "Nigger! Nigger! Nigger!"

The words stung, and Jack fired back that she was "nothing but a cracker."

Unfazed, the girl shot off a rhyme: "Soda cracker's good to eat, nigger's only good to beat."

Hearing the commotion, her father burst through their front door, picked up a rock, and hurled it at Jack.

Jack found his own rock and threw a fastball right back.

The battle waged on until the man's wife ran out of the house and scolded her husband for such immature behavior. As the man skulked back inside, Jack stood his ground, fully prepared to fight some more.

Playing sports and battling neighbors required a lot of energy, and Jack had quite the appetite. His usual treat was a piece of stale bread dunked in water with a bit of sugar. But food was scarce in the Robinson home, and the kids often rummaged through the cupboards without much success.

Mallie sometimes carried home leftovers from the meals she made for the Dodges. The milkman helped, too. He liked the "Robinson

Mallie Robinson and her children—from left to right, Mack, Jack, Edgar, Willa Mae, and Frank—in 1925

Crusoe" family, as some neighbors called them, and gave them unsold milk at the end of the day. A baker also offered them leftover bread and desserts.

When the Robinsons did have extra food, Mallie shared it with her neighbors, even with those who had opposed her move onto Pepper Street. If there was no food in the house, she sent Jack and Willa Mae to school without lunch.

"We would get to school so hungry we could hardly stand up, much less think about our lessons," Jack later said. But two kind teachers, Miss Gilbert and Miss Haney, noticed the problem and made extra sandwiches to share.

As always, Jack ate his lunch fast and ran off to join any game in progress. But he long remembered the sacrifices made by his mother and teachers. One day, he would be just like them.

Bean Shooter Sends Youth to Hospital

Frank Robinson, 15, 121 Pepper street, was given first aid treatment in the emergency hospital Wednesday for lacerations of his throat and cheek, incurred when a bean shooter he was holding in his mouth was forced into the flesh by the sudden closing of a door.

During Jack's childhood, all his brothers went to the hospital for various emergencies. (Pasadena Post, July 8, 1927)

THREE

STOKING THE FIRE

Running in the various heats some remarkable times were created. In the junior 50 yard dash, Jack Robinson of Washington and Willis Fallis of Madison equalled the city record. Eddie Arnold of

This April 17, 1929, article about a citywide elementary school track championship marks the first time Jack's name appeared in the Pasadena Post. *It describes his winning performance in a preliminary heat.*

The track-and-field meet for Pasadena's elementary schools was a festive occasion in 1929. Pasadena Junior College hosted the popular event, and twenty-five buglers in white uniforms and red sashes signaled the start of every competition.

Ten-year-old Jack Robinson represented Washington Elementary in the fifty-yard dash. He had transferred to the school from Cleveland Elementary, and he was well-known among his peers as a fierce competitor and a fast runner.

Jack crouched down and positioned his feet right where he wanted them.

"Runners!" shouted the referee. "Take your mark! Set!"

Bang!

Jack exploded off the line, dug his sneakers into the gray cinders, and flew down his lane, arms pumping, muscles flexing, head up.

When he crossed the finish line, his friends from Washington no doubt roared their support. Not only did Jack capture first place; he also set a record of 6.25 seconds.

Just a month after this record-breaking run, Jack won the gold medal in a school competition that tested performance in the fifty-yard dash, the long jump, and the ball throw. He won that same medal again at Washington in the following year, and he set yet another record at the citywide track meet.

According to the *Pasadena Post*, "A cold wind with threatening rain hampered the athletes and prevented them from breaking records. In the course of the meet, but one new record was established which came in the intermediate soccer throw for distance, when Jack Robinson of Washington broke the old record of 68 feet with a throw of 68 feet, 9 inches."

Jack's athletic prowess extended to other sports, too. In 1930, he led Washington to an undefeated record in the city's indoor baseball league. When the *Post* reported on the stellar season, they listed his first name, in quotation marks, as "Jackie," marking the first time that the paper referred to him that way; they usually called him "Jack."

He was also a star player on Washington's basketball team, which lost the city championship to rival Jefferson Elementary by a score of 18 to 13. "Both teams were probably the best ever developed in Pasadena elementary schools," wrote the *Post*.

By the time he left Washington Elementary, anyone who followed sports in Pasadena knew that Jack Robinson was an outstanding all-around athlete.

WHAT HAPPENED TO EDGAR?

Can you make sense of the story below? What does it tell you about Edgar? About the Pasadena police officers? About the writer of the story? Does it help you understand Jack's life?

STOLEN BALL SENDS YOUTH TO HOSPITAL

Edgar Robinson Defeated in Pre-Season Fight Over 'Pigskin'

'SUBSTITUTE' IS HERO

Joe Straub, in Fast Play, Aids Police Capture Fugitive

Undoubtedly the most exciting pre-season football skirmish in the history of Pasadena occurred today when Edgar Robinson, 17-year-old negro, broke through a line of defense in John's Bike shop, grabbed a football from the show window and tore through an open field on Fair Oaks avenue for what appeared to be a certain touch down.

Guards Tackle Low

Distracted "linesmen" on the bicycle team dashed across the street to the police station, where they notified "Quarterback" Murphy, who in turn called signals which brought running guards, Joe Rodman and Harry Cheek, into a sweeping defense maneuver.

By this time Robinson had gained considerable yardage. A gallant tackle was made by Cheek on the bicycle's 45-yard line and the two opposing "players" bit the asphalt. Cheek, who was conducting himself under the American football rules, was surprised when Robinson turned around and clawed the officer's face with his finger nails. The ball carrier jumped to his feet again and was running for what appeared to be six points when who should tear around the corner, hip pocket dipping sand, but Joe Straub, Catalina Island agent, wearing the colors of the bicycle aggregation.

One Down, 10 on Top

Straub made a flying tackle and both players fell heavily on the sidewalk. The ball was downed on the bicycle's 10-yard line. Robinson applied the same scratching tactics on Straub and was working himself free when Cheek, Rodman and Cliff Farmer piled on.

The game ended with one down and "ten on top."

Robinson was escorted from the field to the psychopathic ward in Los Angeles, while Cheek and Straub were feted at the emergency hospital.

The game ended with the ball in the bicycle shop's possession.

(*Pasadena Evening Post*, July 30, 1928)

Jack was not an exceptional student. His typical grades at Washington Elementary were Bs and Cs, though they dropped lower at times, and a school administrator who evaluated his academic record wrote "Gardener" on a form asking about Jack's probable job in the future.

Jack simply wasn't interested in using his fierce, competitive spirit for classroom work. That remained true when he attended Washington Junior High School, where he continued to excel in every sport he played.

But Jack was willing to take odd jobs—delivering newspapers, mowing grass, watering shrubs, and running errands—so that he could help Mallie pay the bills. It was difficult for him to see his mother struggling to make ends meet, and he often faulted his absent father for the family's financial distress.

"I could only think of him with bitterness," Jack recalled. "He had no right to desert my mother and five children."

Meanwhile, Mallie continued to share whatever she could with people in need. She was a faithful member of the Scattergood Association, which helped Black children living in poverty, and she opened her home to family members in need.

While he admired his mother's sacrifices, Jack resented those who seemed to take advantage of her generosity. Life during the Great Depression—a worldwide economic crisis marked by poverty and unemployment that lasted from 1929 to 1939—was tough enough without the extra burdens.

But then life got tougher.

Jack smelled something burning around 11:30 P.M. on August 18, 1933. The other members of his family did, too, and before long, thick smoke filled the downstairs of their home.

The source of the fire was an old-fashioned woodburning stove in the kitchen. Somehow, the stove's flames had found their way into the walls around the chimney and were reaching toward the roof.

Landmark Is Periled By Flames

Fire starting from an old-fashioned woodburning stove at 11:30 o'clock last night for a time threatened the destruction of one of the oldest residences on the northside. The house stands at 121 Pepper street and is occupied by Mrs. Mallie Robinson.

An excerpt from the front-page article on the fire at 121 Pepper Street (Pasadena Post, August 19, 1933)

The Robinsons ran outside and waited for help to arrive on the scene. The quick response of the fire department prevented the house from being engulfed in flames. The family was shaken, but their home was still livable, with most of the damage confined to the kitchen and the rear part of the house.

The following day, the *Post* reported on the fire, saying that the "venerable residence," one of the oldest in North Pasadena, was "occupied by Mrs. Mallie Robinson."

But Jack and his siblings knew the truth. Their mother was not merely an occupant of 121 Pepper Street—she was its rightful owner. And it was not merely a "venerable residence"—it was "the Castle," as all the Robinson kids called it.

After the fire, Mallie devoted some of her income to home repairs, but she also made sure to stash away some coins here and there for special occasions.

While many of Jack's friends no doubt wished they had his athletic skills, he also envied them for the new clothes they wore at special times. As the youngest in a poor family, Jack was a walking hand-me-down, the recipient of shoes and clothes worn by his older brothers. Birthdays and holidays often passed by without so much as a new shirt.

It was different when Jack graduated from Washington Junior High School. It was one of the happiest days of Mallie's life. She had attended school only through the sixth grade, and she wanted to show him just how proud she was of his accomplishments.

Jack was shocked when he opened his graduation gift. "Through some miracle, she was able to get me my first real suit," he explained years later.

"I remember I cried a little when I saw it."

THE PASADENA KLAN

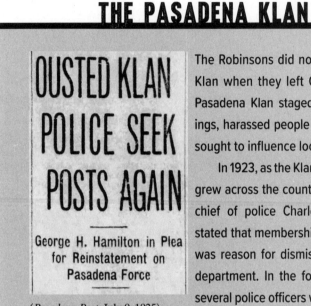

OUSTED KLAN POLICE SEEK POSTS AGAIN

George H. Hamilton in Plea for Reinstatement on Pasadena Force

(*Pasadena Post*, July 9, 1925)

The Robinsons did not escape the Klan when they left Georgia. The Pasadena Klan staged cross burnings, harassed people of color, and sought to influence local politics.

In 1923, as the Klan's popularity grew across the country, Pasadena chief of police Charles H. Kelley stated that membership in the Klan was reason for dismissal from the department. In the following year, several police officers were fired for being Klansmen.

According to the *Pasadena Post*, at least one officer, George Hamilton, was later reinstated. Others were also permitted to return to the force. This means that the Robinsons probably faced Klan members, former Klan members, and Klan supporters in their various encounters with the Pasadena police force.

There weren't a lot of places where Jack could wear his suit, but one of them was Scott Methodist Church, the all-Black church the family attended every Sunday.

Jack did not like going to church, and he protested to Mallie that he could be a good person without showing up for Sunday morning worship. But she would have none of it. Mallie lived and breathed her faith, and she often used it to teach life lessons.

Perhaps her most important lesson centered on the biblical story of Adam and Eve. In Mallie's telling, Adam and Eve were originally Black people, but they turned "pale," or white as ghosts, when God caught them eating from the forbidden tree in the Garden of Eden.

Mallie used this story to teach young Jack that his dark skin was part of God's original design for humanity. It was a blessing, a mark of honor and dignity. With his mother's guidance, Jack grew deeply proud of his Blackness, and he used his racial pride to fuel his lifelong passion for justice.

Ten-year-old Jack was the batboy for the Pasadena Buicks, a semiprofessional team that played at Brookside Park.

FOUR

TARRING JIM CROW

I t was another scorching-hot summer day, and Jack and his friends fumed as they stood outside the fence, watching white kids splashing and jumping and diving.

The Brookside Plunge was usually off-limits to them. Pasadena's white leaders permitted kids of color to swim at the public pool only on Tuesdays. The leaders referred to this day as "International Day." The name was code for anyone who wasn't white—Black Americans, Asian Americans, and Latino Americans, for example. It also

The Brookside Plunge on an "International Day" in 1933

suggested that all people of color were from another country. At the end of the day, workers drained, scrubbed, and refilled the pool for white people to enjoy the rest of the week. The city made it seem that Jack and his friends carried infectious diseases just because of their skin color.

Dejected, the gang often headed to the nearby reservoir, the city's main source of drinking water. Swimming there was prohibited, but that didn't stop the gang from stripping off their clothes, dashing to the water, and splashing around just like the white kids at Brookside Plunge. Jack couldn't swim well, so he was extra careful in the water.

The cool-downs were typically fun, but one day white police officers showed up and started shouting about "niggers" swimming in the drinking water.

The kids thought of bolting, but the sight of officers with drawn guns quickly squelched that idea. All sixteen gang members were "escorted to jail at gunpoint," as Jack recalled, and later released without being charged.

It was Jack's first experience with police officers turning their weapons on him, and it wouldn't be his last.

During his teen years, Jack was an active member of the Pepper Street Gang. "Our gang," he explained, "was made up of blacks, Japanese, and Mexican kids; all of us came from poor families and had extra time on our hands."

It wasn't a violent gang, but it wasn't a harmless club formed for the good of the community, either. As Jack described it, "We threw dirt clods at cars; we hid out on the local golf course and snatched any balls that came our way and often sold them back to their recent owners; we swiped fruit from stands and ran off in a pack; we snitched what we could from the local stores." The gang also smashed windows, broke street lamps, and threw firecrackers.

"All the time," Jack added, "we were aware of a growing resentment at being deprived of some of the advantages that white kids had."

The feeling of resentment stemmed from Jim Crow—laws and customs designed to segregate people of color from white people. Jack and his friends deeply resented the racial discrimination and prejudice that existed throughout the city. They also fought against it, and not just by swimming in the reservoir or stealing food and golf balls.

One day, Jack and his friend Ray Bartlett visited a downtown store and sat at a lunch counter that catered only to white people. When they tried to place their order, servers either ignored them or told them that they didn't wait on Black people.

Jack and Ray were furious, but they stayed on their stools.

As white customers came and went, the teenagers refused to leave. More white customers came and went. Still, Jack and Ray sat.

Finally, after a very long time, the server surrendered and took their order, bringing a successful end to the gang's first sit-in. It wasn't exactly like the protests made popular by Black students in the 1960s—planned, deliberate, and strategic—but it was still a full-fledged sit-in.

On other occasions, Jack protested segregation at the local movie theater.

Although the theater was willing to sell tickets to the Pepper Street Gang, ushers always directed the teens to the balcony, reserving the first level for white patrons. Like the rest of the gang, Jack followed directions and headed up the stairs. But he really wanted one of the best seats available, an eye-level one, not one where he had to look down at the screen.

So he would bide his time, eating popcorn and joking around with his friends, and just when the management dimmed the lights for the start of the movie, he sneaked down the steps and found a choice seat among the white moviegoers. Sometimes, if he got caught and refused to move back to the balcony, he got kicked out.

JIM CROW

A print titled "Jim Crow," probably from between 1835 and 1845

Jim Crow laws and customs are named after "Jim Crow," a Black American character ridiculed in minstrel shows in the 1830s. Minstrel actors were white but painted their faces black and sang and danced in a way that made fun of Black people, especially their speaking patterns. White actor Thomas Dartmouth Rice was the most famous minstrel actor in the 1830s, and he made Black people appear to be buffoons.

After the Civil War, white supremacists used the phrase "Jim Crow" to describe the laws and customs they created to keep Black people from exercising their constitutional rights. These written and unwritten codes required racial segregation in neighborhoods, movie theaters, hospitals, libraries, restaurants, and cemeteries, among many other places. There were separate elevators, taxis, hotels, public bathrooms, blood banks, schools, and churches. Facilities for Black people were far inferior to those for white people. If Black Americans broke Jim Crow codes, they faced arrest. White supremacists also used intimidation, violence, and lynching to enforce Jim Crow.

The Pepper Street Gang encountered Jim Crow elsewhere in Pasadena, too. Although their schools were racially integrated, all their teachers were white, and some were so prejudiced that they excluded kids of color from certain activities.

Their parents or caregivers were also typically stuck in low-paying jobs, unable to secure the better ones held by white people, and their homes were often in the poorer sections of the city, separated from white and wealthier neighborhoods.

Owing to their frequent brushes with the law, the Pepper Street Gang also discovered that every officer in the Pasadena police department was white—and that some of them used every racial slur in the book.

Everywhere they looked, the gang saw white adults in power and white kids with many more privileges than they had. The closer the gang looked, the more they saw, and the more they saw, the more they resented Jim Crow and its supporters, including one particularly racist man in Jack's own neighborhood.

Unlike the many neighbors who had grown to like the Robinsons,

Because Jack was Black, he was not allowed to join the Pasadena YMCA, pictured here in about 1937.

this one never warmed up to them. He was obnoxious and confrontational, and he threw countless racist barbs in their direction. He was also quite fastidious about his lawn.

At one point, a Pepper Street Gang member, possibly Jack, noticed the man carefully tending to sod he had just laid in the front yard. The gang member then met up with his friends and told them what he'd seen.

Inspiration struck. The gang decided to exact revenge, and they soon found a container of tar—the thick, black, sticky substance that people use to seal driveways and roofs. Then, when no one was around, the gang spread the tar all over the man's new sod.

The white neighbor grew livid when he saw the black tar smeared on his new green sod. Suspecting Jack was the culprit, he marched over to the Robinsons' house and threatened Mallie that he would call the police if she didn't make her son repair the damage.

When Mallie confronted Jack, he said he couldn't identify the real culprit. Stymied by her own son, she then contacted the gang members' parents, and they all agreed that the teens should make things right.

Mallie called the gang together, scolded them, and told them to remove the tar.

"How we going to get it off?" they complained.

"I don't care," Mallie said. "Just get it off."

To ensure that they carried out her orders, Mallie stood watch as they cut the tarred grass with scissors or used rags and kerosene to clean it.

Mallie worried about Jack. While she understood that he was rightly resentful of discrimination, she wished that he would channel his anger not into vandalism but into schoolwork. But, as always, Jack continued to choose sports over studies.

PART II

FROM COLLEGE TO THE ARMY

FIVE

SNATCHING SACKS

Jackie Robinson

Robert Chastain

Jack, second row, with his Muir Tech baseball team

J ack Robinson—star catcher and shortstop for John Muir Technical
High School—took a casual lead off third base, his eyes peeled on
the pitcher from archrival Covina High School.

The pitcher stared back, and Jack extended his lead, holding his
arms out as if to balance himself, dancing back and forth, and leaning
toward home plate.

Flustered, the pitcher looked at his catcher, then at Jack, then the
catcher.

Seizing the moment, Jack dropped his arms, sped down the chalk
line, and slid hard into home, right leg first.

"Safe!" yelled the umpire.

That was one of five bases that Jack stole in the six-inning game. It was a remarkable feat that echoed his performance in the same tournament a year earlier, when he'd been "the champion sack snatcher," as one sportswriter put it.

This same writer also referred to the base-stealing champion as "Jack 'Smoky' Robinson." The nickname "Smoky" signaled to readers that Jack was a Black player, but for those who knew him well, it also suggested that his base-running left behind a cloud of dust so thick that no one knew where he was—until he was safe.

At Muir Tech, Jack also earned high praise for his performance in track-and-field competitions, where he focused on the long jump. He loved the explosiveness of the event. "You [toe] the line and spring forward with all your strength," he explained. "Then you jump—you really try to jump off the earth and your legs churn the air like you wanted to reach the moon."

In his first track season, Jack competed against his big brother Mack, the school's star long jumper and the holder of the state record in the hundred-yard dash.

"If there was one person Jack idolized growing up, it was his brother Mack," recalled their sister, Willa Mae, who was also good at sports.

After Mack graduated from high school, he won a spot on the US Olympic track team and traveled to Berlin for the 1936 Summer Olympics. The Robinson family stayed in Pasadena, but they gathered around the radio for live broadcasts.

On August 5, Mack competed in the final race of the 200-meter dash. Under the watchful eye of Adolf Hitler—the German leader who believed Black people were better dead than alive—Mack finished second, winning the silver medal, ahead of his white competitors but just behind Black sprinter Jesse Owens of Ohio State University, who would end up winning four gold medals at the games.

Hitler was angry, but the Robinsons were thrilled.

Jack eclipsed Mack's star at Muir Tech by becoming an all-around athlete, exceptional in every sport he played.

In tennis, he captured the junior boys' singles championship in the Pacific Coast Negro Tennis Tournament, crushing his opponent by a score of 6–1, 6–2.

During basketball season, sportswriters referred to him as the "colored flash," the "dusky sharpshooter," and "black lightning"— phrases that captured both the color of his skin and his remarkable skills.

And then there was football season, when a sportswriter described him as "the best passer and field general in Muir history."

Because he was so well-known, Jack was often targeted. Some opposing players trash-talked to him, using racial slurs, and others took cheap shots.

The worst hit came in his last high school football game, when Muir Tech squared off against Glendale High School before ten thousand screaming fans at the Rose Bowl, Pasadena's famous sports stadium.

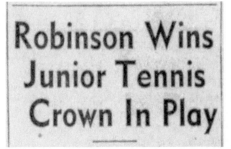

Robinson Wins Junior Tennis Crown In Play

Jack captured first place in the junior division (fifteen to eighteen years old) of the Pacific Coast Negro Tennis Tournament in 1936. (Pasadena Post, September 7, 1936)

Jack in his Muir Tech track jersey

In the first quarter, just as Muir was about to score a touchdown, three Glendale defensive players "piled on" Jack after he'd already been tackled. The unsportsmanlike act left him with two broken ribs and forced him to the sidelines for the rest of the game. Without their star player, Muir lost 20–0.

Two months later, Jack came roaring back, this time on the basketball court. In the last game of the season—and his last high school sports event—he scored twenty-one points.

"The game was rough throughout," a reporter noted, "and numerous fouls were called, most of them on Muir Tech."

Jack Robinson gave as good as he got.

This signature in his senior yearbook indicates that Jack referred to himself as "Jack," not "Jackie."

A rare photo of Jack sporting a mustache at Pasadena Junior College

SIX

BANDING WITH BLACK BULLDOGS

J ack enrolled at Pasadena Junior College (PJC) on February 1, 1937, just a few days after graduating from Muir Tech. PJC was close to home, and the tuition was free. Plus, it had an excellent sports program.

During the next two years, Jack played hard to extend his reputation as an outstanding all-around athlete. In baseball season, he became the area's top base stealer. An early game saw him stealing second, third, and home, an accomplishment he repeated throughout his time on PJC's diamond.

Jack's star at PJC shone most brightly on the football field, but only after he squashed an eruption of racism on his own team.

White PJC players from Oklahoma felt so superior to some of their Black teammates that they refused to play with them. Jack was slated to be PJC's starting quarterback, and as the *Black* team leader, he would not tolerate racial abuse against any Black player.

Jack went to coach Tom Mallory and delivered a threat—either order the Oklahomans to stop their bigoted behavior or Jack and his good friend Ray Bartlett, another Black star, would transfer to rival Compton Junior College. The threat was powerful, and Mallory acted quickly.

"Coach Mallory laid down the law and the Oklahoma fellows

Jackie Robinson, the versatile athlete at Pasadena junior college, who was leading basketball scorer in the western division and leaped to a new national jaysee record in the broadjump last Saturday at Claremont, is considered the greatest college baseball player in America today . . . but he will never play professional baseball in the Coast or major leagues . . . because he is a negro . . . if you have race prejudices, we still say it's a doggoned shame . . . Jack, you'll remember, won two medals for most stolen bases in the 20-30 club invitation baseball tournament here a couple of years ago when he played with Muir Tech high school.

Sports columnist Dave Meikeljohn writes that Jack will never play in Major League Baseball. (Pomona Progress Bulletin, May 10, 1938)

became more than decent," Jack recalled.

While the PJC coach helped resolve the team's racial crisis, Jack faced another crisis when he sprained an ankle and chipped a bone in his right leg during a preseason practice. With his leg in a cast, he could only watch as PJC suffered four consecutive losses.

After a month, his cast came off, and Jack became the star of PJC's dreams. As the starting quarterback, punter, and kicker, he led the team to an undefeated record for the remainder of the regular season.

On Thanksgiving Eve 1937, the PJC Bulldogs faced the Caltech Beavers in the city championship game. Eighteen thousand loud fans at the Rose Bowl were spellbound as Jack steered the Bulldogs to a 12–0 victory. A writer described the star as "a dark-hued phantom of the gridiron" whose "brilliant running and passing" were the keys to victory.

At the beginning of 1938, Jack's final year at PJC, he was the basketball team's lead scorer. Once again, he attracted more than his fair share of fouls from opposing players.

As usual, Jack hit back. In one game, he head-butted the face of a player who had been picking on him. The result was a lot of blood on the court, and it wasn't Jack's.

JACK ROBINSON (Acting Captain).

Jack continued to sign his name as "Jack" in the 1939 Pasadena Junior College yearbook.

More blood spilled when he faced off against guard Sam Babich in a game against Long Beach Junior College. Babich targeted him, Jack fired back, and the two players fouled each other as much as they could in the closing minutes of the game.

After PJC clinched the win, Babich asked Jack if he wanted to fight. Jack said yes, and he soon felt a right hook to the face. Jack immediately flew into Babich, knocking him to the floor and straddling and pummeling him.

Then, according to the *Post*, "nearly all the people in the gym began swinging at the nearest person, friend or foe." With help from coaches, local police officers finally stopped the melee. No one was arrested, but soon enough, Jack would land in jail.

Later that month, Jack and his friend Jonathan Nolan went to see a movie in downtown Pasadena. As they later strolled down the sidewalk, Nolan began to sing a popular tune called "Flat Foot Floogie."

It was a happy scene—until they walked by a white police officer who, for unclear reasons, took personal offense at Nolan's singing. The officer angrily confronted the two friends, and because they felt unfairly provoked, they protested and resisted.

That led to their arrest and a night in the city jail. Jack now had a police record, and he subsequently received a suspended jail sentence of ten days.

Jack's final year at PJC took a favorable turn during the overlapping baseball and track seasons.

In his favorite track event—the long jump—he did the unthinkable when he leaped twenty-five feet, six and a half inches, a distance that set the national junior college record.

In baseball, he batted .417, stole twenty-five bases, and crossed home

Jack Robinson Leads Pasadena To Victory

BY GEORGE GARNER

PASADENA, Calif., Nov. 4.—The greatest football throng in the Rose Bowl history to see a junior college game, estimated at 50,000, wildly cheered the sensational playing of Jack Robinson, Pasadena Junior college's astonishing back.

Robinson made his historical showing before a crowd that set a new high in national junior collegiate attendance records, gathered to witness the Pasadena Junior college vs. Compton junior college fight for the Southern California junior college championship.

Jack Robinson was responsible for all of Pasadena's points—making 14 himself and passing to Red Robinshon to make the remaining six points.

Robinson started his team off on their 20-7 win by taking the Compton kickoff on his own 11-yard line and racing to the 44. A short gain found Robinson feinting to pass and making his way around his own right end for a first down on the Compton 27 yard line. Jack succeeded in bringing the score to a tie. An intercepted pass by Jack put the ball on Compton's 29 after running it back 51 yards. Robinson netted ten yards on the first play to toss a flat pass to Red Robinson, 14 yards and the second tally.

It was late in the half that Robinson ran 45 yards for a touchdown.

Jack is a brother to famous Olympic star, Mack Robinson, now setting new records at Oregon State.

Jack attracted national attention during his football career at PJC. This article appeared in the Chicago Defender, *one of the largest Black newspapers in the country, on November 5, 1938.*

plate forty-three times. The *Pomona Progress Bulletin* reported that Jack was "considered the greatest college baseball player in America today."

Chicago White Sox manager Jimmy Dykes had an opportunity to watch Jack's skills on March 14. His Major League Baseball team had come to Pasadena to play local youths in an exhibition game to raise money for a baseball camp.

After seeing Jack steal bases and turn a double play, Dykes said, "Geez, if that kid was white, I'd sign him right now."

Once again, Jack's reputation grew by leaps and bounds during football season. As his star status rose, so did the popularity of PJC's sporting events. In the 1938 season, his spectacular play resulted in record-setting attendance in national junior college sports.

As one writer described the scene at a November game, "The greatest football throng in Rose Bowl history to see a junior college game, estimated at 50,000, cheered the sensational playing of Jack Robinson, Pasadena Junior College's astonishing back."

But once again, Jack's popularity and talent did not protect him from racism.

When the PJC Bulldogs traveled to Phoenix, Arizona, the Black players discovered that their sleeping arrangements were racially segregated.

"We weren't allowed to stay in the same hotel with the rest of the team, with the white players," Ray Bartlett recalled. "We had to stay in a place that was like a house converted to a hotel."

Jack and his friends refused the rooms and instead stayed awake all night, fuming about the injustice and planning to make sure it would never happen again. Despite the racism, or perhaps because of it, Jack and his teammates played on to victory.

By the end of the season, Jack was the top football prospect on the Pacific coast. Major universities came knocking on his door, and after graduating in January 1939, he announced his choice.

SEVEN

RESISTING ARREST

On January 2, 1939, the city of Pasadena held its annual Tournament of Roses Parade, a spectacular event with colorful bands, cowboys on horses, and floats decorated with flowers galore.

Edgar, Jack's oldest sibling, saw it as an occasion to make money, and he placed folding chairs along the parade route, hoping to rent them out for four or five dollars each.

As he was minding his business, two police officers approached and asked what he was doing. Edgar replied that he had purchased a license for renting chairs, and he began to dig into his pocket for the document.

At this point, according to his account, one of the officers knocked him to the ground. Edgar fought back and ended up with a bruised arm, a black eye, and his hands in cuffs.

When he later protested his treatment to Pasadena's chief of police, the chief allegedly ordered him to get out of his office "before you are clubbed on the head."

The local branch of the National Association for the Advancement of Colored People (NAACP) learned about the incident and registered a formal protest with the Board of City Directors. Although board members failed to take any punitive action against the police department, they learned once again that the Robinson family would never go away quietly when facing injustice, especially police brutality.

THE NAACP

The NAACP protests lynching at a crime conference in Washington, DC, on December 11, 1934.

In 1908, a white mob in Springfield, Illinois, erupted in violence after learning that two Black prisoners had been transferred to another jail for their personal safety. The mob torched Black homes and businesses and murdered at least two Black people. In response to the anti-Black violence in Springfield and elsewhere, an interracial group of activists created the National Association for the Advancement of Colored People (NAACP) on February 12, 1909.

The mission of the new civil rights group was "to promote equality of rights and eradicate caste or race prejudice among citizens of the United States; to advance the interest of colored citizens; to secure for them impartial suffrage; and to increase their opportunities for securing justice in the courts, education for their children, employment according to their ability, and complete equality before the law."

By the time Jack was born, the NAACP had about ninety thousand members and more than three hundred local branches. The organization established a national reputation as a legal and legislative advocate for Black civil rights. Its early campaigns against the Ku Klux Klan, lynching, and police brutality received widespread attention.

The Pasadena branch of the NAACP was established in 1919, and within five years it had attracted about 140 members. The branch advocated for equality, fought against police brutality, and challenged racial segregation in public facilities, including the Brookside Plunge.

In February 1939, Jack enrolled in the Extension Division of the University of California at Los Angeles (UCLA). He decided to attend UCLA because of its high-quality sports program and because it was near his family, especially his brother Frank, Jack's biggest supporter and strongest defender. Twenty-seven-year-old Frank worked as a tree trimmer for Pasadena. The job didn't pay well, and he and his family lived with the other Robinsons at 121 Pepper Street. It was not an ideal arrangement, but it allowed Frank and Jack to remain close.

Throughout the spring, Jack studied hard to complete the courses he needed to enroll full-time at UCLA's main campus: French, geometry, and algebra.

When summer arrived, he shifted his focus back to sports, clinching yet another tennis title. One writer said he played with a "wickedly unorthodox style, characterized by lightning speed, and uncanny judgment."

Shortly after the victory, tragedy struck. Frank died from injuries sustained in a motorcycle accident.

When he heard the news, Jack collapsed onto his bed at home and sobbed. "I was very shaken up by his death," he recalled. "It was hard to believe he was gone, hard to believe I would no longer have his support."

Jack no doubt missed hearing Frank's cheers a month later when he led the Pasadena Sox, an interracial team sponsored by the Chicago White Sox, to victory in the Southern California Amateur Baseball championship game. One of three Black players on the team, Jack slugged four hits and stole home plate.

The combined play of the Black teammates offered "the biggest argument for the participation of the Negro in major league baseball," remarked the *California Eagle*.

Yet again, though, Jack discovered that his athletic prowess did not protect him from racism in Pasadena. After a softball game in early September, just before he was about to head to UCLA, Jack climbed behind the wheel of his 1931 Plymouth. Several friends also jumped on the car's exterior running boards and held on tight as Jack drove through town.

Before long, a white driver pulled alongside Jack and said something derogatory about "niggers." Ray Bartlett, one of the friends on the running boards, leaned over and used his glove to whack the man in the face.

When the angry man sped away, Jack followed him to a stop, hopped out of the car, and prepared to fight. But the man backed down, especially when he noticed a crowd of Black youths gathering around the two cars.

That did not end the situation. After the man drove off, white Pasadena police officer John C. Hall pulled up on his motorcycle and sought to arrest anyone still in the area.

Jack's friends, including Bartlett, ducked away. "But not Jack," Bartlett recalled. "He just wouldn't back down. He was just stubborn."

Officer Hall unharnessed his gun.

"I found myself up against the side of my car, with a gun barrel pressed unsteadily into the pit of my stomach," Jack said. "I was scared to death."

Jack spent the night in jail, charged with blocking traffic and resisting arrest.

Help eventually came in the form of UCLA officials who did not want to lose their star athlete during the upcoming football season. They arranged for him to plead guilty in absentia, paid his fine for being absent in court, and secured a sentence that suspended additional time in jail. A week later, they arranged for a publicity shoot with Jack showing off his moves on the gridiron and posing for the camera (see football image on page 53).

"I got out of that trouble because I was an athlete," Jack said.

Of course, he had gotten *into* that same trouble because he was a proud Black man who refused to back down in the face of a racist slur.

When Los Angeles sportswriters first learned that Jack would join UCLA's football program, they were thrilled. But as Jack would experience throughout his career, their enthusiasm didn't prevent them from often making reference to Jack's skin color in their articles about his playing and peppering their writing with offensive nicknames and imagery.

Frank Finch of the *Los Angeles Times* described Jack as "the juiciest plum of the 1939 crop of college-bound athletes" and as a "jittery jack rabbit." Finch added that if UCLA coach Babe Horrell played Jack in the backfield with Black quarterback Kenny Washington, "UCLA will boast two dark angels of destruction at the same time."

Paul Zimmerman, another *Times* sportswriter, agreed that Jack was a star, but he described him in hurtful language, using a stereotype of Black people as watermelon thieves. "All Jackie did at [PJC] was throw with ease and accuracy, punt efficiently, and run with that ball like it was a watermelon and the guy who owned it was after him with a shotgun."

Racist insults also came from opposing teams and their fans. Jack swallowed the slurs and lived up to the hype. As UCLA's starting halfback, he averaged about twelve yards per carry and helped lead the Bruins to an undefeated season, including a tie game against their archrival, the University of Southern California, before a crowd of 103,000.

Throughout the season, sportswriters lavished his skills on offense with the highest praise possible. They described him as "Jackie 'Jumping Jive' Robinson," "a positive menace," "the Brown phantom," "Jackie the Jitterbug," "the halfback with wings on his feet," "the fastest man in college football," and "the greatest half-back in America." Gerald Oliver, the coach of the Oregon Ducks, added to the heap of praise. "You need mechanized cavalry to stop him," he said.

Sportswriters were less positive with regard to his play on defense. "As a blocker he is in the same class with Shirley Temple," wrote the *Los Angeles Daily News*, comparing him to the famous child movie star. The *Los Angeles Times* criticized him as "no tack-ler" after one game, adding, "Jack Robinson looked woefully weak defensively."

At the end of the season, the *California Eagle* observed that Jack was an excellent candidate for professional football or Major League

> Pasadena claims Robinson can do everything with a football but eat it, and if it had a green cover and a red heart, he could do that, too. At any rate, he was the most bally-hooed player in the minor circuits on the coast last fall.

Sportswriter Robert Myers describes Jack by using a stereotype of Black people as watermelon lovers. (*Pomona Progress Bulletin*, September 26, 1939)

Baseball. More stunning was the *Eagle*'s prediction that Jack "may go on to hand Battler Jim Crow the beating of his life." Little did the paper know just how right it would turn out to be.

Jackie Robinson has changed his major at U. C. L. A. from physical education to history . . . reason: he had to take science as a physical ed student but not with a history major . . . "I never could get that science stuff," he explains . . .

Jack focused on sports over studies throughout his years in school. (Pasadena Post, March 14, 1940)

Jack's star at UCLA climbed higher during basketball season. His "black magic" on the court, his "speedy dribbling dashes," his "eagle eye," and his outstanding "body control and judgment of distance" resulted in at least one sportswriter dubbing him "the best basketball player in the United States."

Jack shot to the top among all scorers in the Southern District of the Pacific Coast Conference, beating out the University of Southern California's forward Ralph Vaughn, whom *Life* magazine had called the "player of the year."

Baseball season, however, was another story. At PJC, Robinson had played so well that a white writer said that "had it not been for the policy prohibiting Negroes in organized baseball he would have been sought by half a dozen major league scouts."

Jack set an NCAA record in the long jump in 1940.

But Jack faltered at UCLA. He was a fantastic base runner, but his pitching and fielding were dismal. No Bruin compiled more errors than Jack. Worst of all, though he started the season with an impressive string of singles and doubles, he batted only .089. "There's nothing major leaguish about that," wrote the *Pasadena Post*.

Away from the diamond, Jack redeemed himself in track and field when he long-jumped twenty-five feet in the Pacific Coast Conference meet after only ten days of practice. It was a new conference record, and shortly after he won the NCAA title in the same event.

By the end of his first year at UCLA, Jack Roosevelt Robinson had earned letters in four varsity sports. Even as a freshman, he was now a sports legend.

WAS JACK THE FIRST?

In addition to lettering in these four sports, Jack also excelled at Ping-Pong and tennis.

The UCLA website claims that James "Cap" Haralson, who attended the university two decades before Jack, "was UCLA's first ever athlete to earn 4 varsity letters in the sports of track and field, football, basketball & baseball." In 2009, he was inducted into the university's Hall of Fame. But the *Los Angeles Times* stated, "Robinson was UCLA's first athlete to win varsity letters in four sports: baseball, basketball, football and track." Rachel Robinson, Jack's widow, also wrote, "One of the greatest athletes in the history of UCLA, Jack was the first to win letters in football, baseball, basketball, and track and field." What might account for this confusion?

EIGHT

FALLING IN LOVE

Rachel sat in her family's old Ford V8, looking in the rearview mirror and wondering when in the world he would arrive.

Finally, Jack whipped into UCLA's parking lot and jumped out of his car. As usual, he was behind schedule and had to make up for lost time.

Gathering her belongings, Rachel watched Jack's path and plotted her own so that she might run into him.

"I was the aggressor, no doubt about it," she said years later.

Seventeen-year-old Rachel Isum commuted to campus from her home on Thirty-Sixth Place, a white-frame cottage in a racially integrated neighborhood. Growing up, she had experienced discrimination at a movie theater and restaurant, but for the most part she felt safe and comfortable in her surroundings.

The Isums were financially stable but far from wealthy. Charles Raymond Isum, Rachel's father, had been gassed so badly in World War I that he had to retire early from his work as a bookbinder with the *Los Angeles Times*. Zellee Isum, Rachel's mother, was a self-employed caterer, and while she provided for the family, she was not able to pay for her daughter's college education. A local civic group awarded Rachel a scholarship so that she could study nursing.

At nearby UCLA, Rachel noticed that Black students tended to hang out together in Kerchoff Hall—and that Jack Robinson held a part-time maintenance job there. She knew Jack was the Big Man on Campus, and she soon found herself attracted to him.

"He was big, he was broad-shouldered, he was very attractive physically, and he had pigeon toes you couldn't miss," she recalled.

There was another quality she found intensely attractive. "He was clearly comfortable and proud of being a black man," she said. "Jack displayed his color by wearing white shirts. There was a kind of dignity about him and a sense of purpose that attracted me."

Ray Bartlett introduced Jack and Rachel, and she sensed they shared a characteristic. "I was extremely shy, but I was rather pleased to see that he was also shy in that encounter," she explained. "However, my impression of him was that he had great self-confidence, and I was pleased to see that he was not arrogant."

Jack was also struck. "I was immediately attracted to Rachel's looks and charm," he remembered. "When she left, I walked to the parking lot with her. She made me feel at ease, and I thoroughly enjoyed talking to her."

They made time to continue their chats in the following weeks. "There are few people it is easy for me to confide in," Jack recalled, "but when I was with Rae I was delighted to find that I could tell her anything. She was always understanding and, beyond that, very direct and honest with me." Jack also discovered that Rachel called him by his real name, Jack, as a term of endearment, and he deeply appreciated that.

In November, Jack asked Rachel to go to the homecoming dance. Rachel was delighted and bought a new black dress and a hat with fur trim. Wearing his only suit, Jack drove her to the swanky Biltmore Hotel in downtown Los Angeles, where they danced to Duke Ellington's "Mood Indigo" and Hoagy Carmichael's "Stardust."

"I was excited and happy and full of anticipation, wondering on the ride home whether he would kiss me," she recalled. "I wanted him to, I really wanted him to kiss me. He pecked me on the cheek. That was all. I was disappointed."

The disappointment didn't last, and the two soon became affectionate and fell in love.

Nevertheless, the strong bond between them didn't prevent Jack from thinking about leaving UCLA before earning his diploma.

Jack and Rachel, shown here in 1951, fell in love while they were students at UCLA.

In early March 1941, Jack played his last basketball game for the UCLA Bruins, and the student body gave him a standing ovation as he walked off the court.

Although he was once again the top scorer in the league, white sportswriters refused to vote him onto the all-conference basketball team. Hank Shatford, the sports editor for UCLA's newspaper, denounced that act as a "flagrant bit of prejudice."

Shortly after, Jack announced that he was leaving UCLA, explaining that he felt the need to provide financial support for his hardworking mother.

"I was aghast," Rachel said. "I tried to talk him out of it. He was so close to finishing." Jack's mentor, Reverend Karl Downs, the pastor of his home church, also sought to dissuade him.

But Jack had used up his eligibility in football and basketball, and he wasn't inclined to stick around any longer. He wasn't a scholar, and he was convinced that a college degree wouldn't help him become a sports coach.

Jack quit school and landed a job as an assistant athletic director with the National Youth Administration (NYA), a government program that provided mentoring and job training for people between the ages of sixteen and twenty-five. Although he loved the job, it didn't last long. World War II was on the horizon, and because the war industry and the army needed young people, the government canceled the program.

With few options, Jack looked toward sports, though that choice was also limited. After all, Major League Baseball and the National Football League enforced informal agreements prohibiting Black participation. But there was one possibility that looked somewhat attractive—semiprofessional football.

In September 1941, though he'd already dropped out of school, Jack was able to play in a college all-star game against the Chicago Bears, an all-white NFL team known for its toughness. His performance was so good that the crowd of 98,200 rocked the stadium with a standing ovation for him at the end of the game. Bears receiver Dick Plasman added, "That Jackie Robinson is the fastest man I've ever seen in uniform."

Still, Jack was denied a chance to play on an NFL team, and by the end of the month, he and his friend Ray Bartlett sailed to Hawaii to play semiprofessional football for the Honolulu Bears. The pay was about a hundred dollars a game, so the two also took construction jobs in nearby Pearl Harbor.

In a show of respect, local sportswriters decided they would not refer to Jack's skin color in their coverage. "We were determined that this man was going to get a chance to make it on his own, without undue pressure," said reporter Jim Becker. The writers also referred to him as "Jack Robinson," not "Jackie Robinson."

Jack played well for the Bears, and on December 5, after the end of their short season, he boarded the SS *Lurline* for the trip back to California. Two days later, when the ship was about a thousand miles from Pearl Harbor, Jack noticed crew members painting all the windows black.

He asked what was going on, and the crew informed him that Japan had just bombed Pearl Harbor and that the captain had ordered them to black out the ship so it could not be easily spotted by Japanese pilots or submarines at night. The United States was now at war with Japan.

Jack "was scared at first but then got into a poker game and forgot all about the war," according to the *Honolulu Star-Bulletin.* But putting the war out of his mind was impossible. Jack would soon face the prospect of serving in the army.

After he left UCLA, Jack, shown here with friends Ray Bartlett, left, and Marion Wildly, center, played semiprofessional football for the Honolulu Bears.

NINE

FIGHTING THE ARMY

JACKIE ROBINSON
Faces old pal Kenny

Bear pros seek ninth straight win

Hollywood's burly Bears, the only undefeated major football team in the west will seek it's ninth straight win Sunday at Gilmore stadium against the Los Angeles Bulldogs. It will be the third meeting of the year between the rival clubs.

Los Angeles has lost only three games this year, two of them to Hollywood. The other loss was a 10-9 defeat to San Francisco which has been doubly avenged with a 21-13 win and a terrific 36-0 victory to date.

Now the Bulldogs, bolstered with the addition of Jackie Robinson, seek revenge for the two Hollywood drubbings.

It will be the first time in history that Robinson has played against Kenny Washington, his former teammate at UCLA.

Back in Pasadena, Jack did not volunteer for the army. He registered for the military draft, but he also requested an exemption from service so that he could support his mother, Mallie.

While he waited for the draft board's decision, he worked as a truck driver and played a few games of professional football with the Los Angeles Bulldogs, a racially mixed team in the Pacific Coast Football League. Then, he did something extra special.

On March 18, 1942, Jack and Nate Moreland, a Black pitcher in the Mexican National League, headed to Brookside Park, where the Chicago White Sox were in spring training.

Jack briefly played for the Los Angeles Bulldogs after returning from Hawaii.
(*Los Angeles Daily News*, December 16, 1941)

Spotting manager Jimmy Dykes, Jack and Moreland strode over and asked for a tryout. The Sox skipper replied by saying that Major League Baseball (MLB) had an "unwritten law" against hiring Black players.

"The matter is out of the hands of us managers," he claimed. "We are powerless to act, and it's strictly up to the club owners and [MLB commissioner] Judge [Kenesaw Mountain] Landis to start the ball a-rolling. Go after them!

"Personally," Dykes added, "I would welcome Negro players on the White Sox, and I believe every one of the other fifteen league managers would do likewise. As for the players, they'd all get along too."

Jack and Moreland protested, arguing that the unwritten law was unfair and that they were good enough to play for the team. Dykes claimed to agree, but he still refused to advocate for their entry into MLB.

According to Black sportswriter Herman Hill, the Sox manager also declined to pose for a photo with them, and "several White Sox players hovered around menacingly with bats in their hands."

Jack and Moreland walked away in disgust.

OUGHT TO BE EASY FOR HIM

Private Jack Robinson, intercollegiate broad jump champion in 1939, finds taking an obstacle course at the Fort Riley, Kans., cavalry replacement training center no trouble at all. Robinson, football, track, basketball, and baseball star from U.C.L.A., was caught taking off across a ditch after scaling the wall and jumping the railing in the background.

The Sox didn't want him, but the US Army did. They denied his request for an exemption, and on April 3, 1942, Jack packed his clothes and reported for military service, as required by the draft.

"I plan to work hard and make the most of my Army training," he said before

Jack initially received a deferment after a physical examination failed to qualify him for service. The army ordered another exam, and he passed that one. (*Chicago Defender*, May 30, 1942)

Heavyweight boxing champion Joe Louis and Jack—shown here in 1946—became close friends at Fort Riley.

leaving for thirteen weeks of basic training.

At Fort Riley in Kansas, he handled the M1 rifle with ease and scored high at the firing range. One eyewitness said he hit the bull's-eye fourteen out of sixteen times. Jack's superiors also evaluated his overall character as "excellent."

Jack applied for Officer Candidate School (OCS), but despite his stellar qualifications, he was far from a shoo-in. Very few Black men became army officers. A bastion of Jim Crow, the US Army practiced racial segregation and relegated most soldiers of color to jobs like cooking and cleaning.

While Jack waited to learn about OCS, he worked as a caretaker of the horses and stables. His morale suffered another blow when he learned that the officer in charge of the baseball team had declared, "I'll break up the team before I'll have a nigger on it."

The one bright spot in his life was his new friendship with a fellow Black soldier—heavyweight boxing champion Joe Louis. The "Brown Bomber" was a popular celebrity and had friends in high places virtually everywhere.

When Jack told Louis that no Black soldier had ever been accepted for OCS at Fort Riley, the champ called an influential contact at the War Department. Soon after that, Jack and several other Black soldiers were admitted to OCS and later commissioned as officers.

THE NAACP AT WAR

During World War II, members of the 93rd Infantry Division were among the first Black foot soldiers to go into action in the South Pacific theater, including troops shown here on Japanese-held Bougainville Island in Papua New Guinea, c. 1944

Before Jack was drafted, NAACP attorney Thurgood Marshall lobbied for racial integration in all sectors of the US military. In a 1940 letter to secretary of war Henry Stimson, Marshall wrote: "The present defense program is being pushed forward for the avowed purpose of protecting democracy in the United States. It is impossible to maintain such a program if the program itself is based upon undemocratic policies such as racial discrimination." Stimson supported racial segregation, and in a letter to Marshall, he wrote: "In accordance with the well-established policy which is endorsed by the colored people, the races have never been mixed within the units of the United States Army." Marshall, of course, did not endorse that policy, and he waged campaigns against it throughout World War II. The US military would not begin to desegregate officially until 1948, long after Jack was honorably discharged.

Second Lieutenant Jack Robinson became the officer in charge of morale among Black soldiers on base. It wasn't an easy job, but he relished the chance to fight for the rights of his fellow soldiers.

One of the first problems he faced was the segregated seating arrangement at the base's restaurant. Black soldiers complained that there were few seats and that they had to wait a long time, even when "whites only" seats were empty.

Jack telephoned his superior with a request for additional seats, but the white major, who didn't realize that Jack was Black, declined.

"Lieutenant, let me put it to you this way," he said. "How would you like to have your wife sitting next to a nigger?"

According to Jack, "Pure rage took over. I was so angry that I asked him if he knew how close his wife had ever been to a nigger. I was shouting at the top of my voice. Every typewriter in headquarters stopped. The clerks were frozen in disbelief at the way I ripped into the major."

Jack filed a complaint about the major's racist comments, and the base soon added more seats for Black soldiers.

In early 1944, Jack was transferred to Camp Hood, forty miles southwest of Waco, Texas, where he was put in charge of a segregated tank platoon that included twenty-five Black soldiers.

Camp Hood, like Fort Riley, was marred by racism. Black soldiers faced segregated and inferior conditions across the camp. If they went off base, they found Jim Crow laws and customs enforced by police officers willing to use whatever methods they deemed necessary.

On July 6, 1944, after visiting a Black officers' club, Jack boarded a bus bound for a military hospital where he was receiving treatment for a bone chip in his right ankle, an old sports injury.

Walking toward the back, Jack saw a friendly face, that of Virginia

Jones, whose husband was also a Black officer. Jack sat next to her in the middle section of the bus, and the two began to chat.

After traveling five or six blocks, the white bus driver, Milton Renegar, glared at Jack and angrily ordered him to the back of the bus, where Blacks were to sit. Renegar might have believed that Jones was white, and that Jack was harassing her.

Jack refused to move. He had probably heard that the army was in the process of issuing a regulation desegregating all military buses.

The bus driver grew impatient, and the two men exchanged angry words. As Jack later described it, "[Renegar] tells me that if I don't move to the rear he will make trouble for me when we get to the bus station, and I told him that was up to him."

The situation escalated when the bus arrived at the station. According to Jack,

> When he got to the bus station a lady got off the bus before I got off, and she tells me that she is going to prefer [file] charges against me. That was a white lady. And I said that's all right, too, I don't care if she prefers charges against me. The bus driver asked for my identification card. I refused to give it to him. He then went to the dispatcher and told him something. What he told him I don't know. He then comes back and tells the people that this nigger is making trouble. I told the bus driver to stop [expletive] with me, so he gets the rest of the men around there and starts blowing his top and someone calls the MP's.

The military police took Jack to a guard room, and there he encountered a white private who referred to him as a "nigger."

Jack shot off a quick reply. "I told him that if he, a private, ever called me that name (a nigger) again I would break him in two."

Jack's blood continued to boil when he dealt with the officers who took sworn statements from eyewitnesses to the bus incident. Captain Gerald Bear, the commander of the military police, said that "Lt. Robinson's attitude in general was disrespectful and impertinent to

little advice. I want to know just how far should go with the case, what I mean is should I appeal to the NAACP and the Negro Press? I don't want any unfavorable publicity for myself or the Army but I believe in fair play and I feel I have to let some one in on the case. If I write the NAACP I hope to get statements from all the witnesses because a broad minded person can see how the people framed me.

You can see sir that I need your advice. I don't care what the outcome of the trial is because I know I am being framed and the charges aren't too bad. I would like get your advice about the publicity. I have a lot of good publicity out and I feel I have numerous friends on the press but I first want to hear from you before I d any thing I will be sorry for later on.

Sir as I said I don't mind trouble but I do believe in fair play and justice. I feel that I'm being take. in this case and I will tell people about it unless the trial is fair. Let me hear from you so I will know what steps to take.

Jack Robinson
LT. Jack Robinson
Ward 11 B
McClosky Gen. Hosp.
Temple Texas

Jack seeks advice about the bus incident from Truman Gibson, a Black civilian assistant to secretary of war Henry Stimson.

his superior officers, and very unbecoming to an officer in the presence of enlisted men."

After taking statements, Bear released Jack, and in the coming days, commanding officers deliberated whether to prosecute him.

Three weeks later, Jack was formally arrested, charged with insubordination, disobeying his superior officers, and using "vile, obscene, and abusive language in a public place."

During his court-martial trial, he sat in the courtroom with shackles on his hands and legs.

When he took the stand and defended his angry reaction to being called a "nigger," a prosecuting attorney asked him whether he even knew what the word meant.

Jack replied, "My Grandmother gave me a good definition, she was a slave, and she said the definition of the word was a low, uncouth person, and pertains to no one in particular; but I don't consider that I am low and uncouth . . . I don't consider myself a nigger at all, I am a negro, but not a nigger."

Jack was acquitted of all charges.

He had fought hard for his personal dignity and for the rights of his fellow Black soldiers, but Jack was now eager to get out of the army, and he sent an official request to be placed on "inactive status" because of his ankle injury.

On November 28, 1944, the US Army relieved him of active duty "by reason of physical disqualification."

Finally, Jack was free. Free from the army. Free from its undemocratic treatment of Black soldiers. Free from having to fight in Europe. And free to fight battles of his own choosing.

PART III

BASEBALL

Discharged before he could fight overseas, Jack battled racial discrimination and prejudice throughout his short-lived army career.

TEN

FUELING THE
NEGRO LEAGUES

Ted Alexander threw a wicked curveball. He had pitched for the Kansas City Monarchs in the Negro Leagues, and though he was now in the army, he practiced when he could.

Jack spotted him on a baseball field at Camp Breckinridge in Kentucky, to which he had been transferred just before his discharge. Before long, the two were playing catch and talking about their futures.

Alexander mentioned that Jack might be able to make a decent salary in the Negro Leagues, and that the Monarchs were searching for players just like him.

Inspired, Jack wrote a letter to Thomas Baird, a co-owner of the Monarchs, asking about the possibility of playing. Baird knew Jack's superstar history, and he replied right away, eventually offering him $400 a month if he made the team during tryouts in April 1945.

Jack was primed to go, but first there was a short detour.

In 1943, Reverend Karl Downs, Jack's longtime mentor, had left Scott Methodist Church in Pasadena to become president of Samuel Huston College in Texas. The school was in dire straits, and he needed help with its athletic program. He turned to his best resource—Jack.

"There was very little money involved, but I knew that Karl would have done anything for me, so I couldn't turn him down," Jack recalled.

For three solid months, from January to March, Jack worked hard to instill enthusiasm for sports among the student body. He also built a basketball team that beat the league champions in a nail-biting finish.

The students loved Jack, and he loved them, but the Monarchs were offering more money. At the end of March, Jack called the basketball team together to announce that he would soon be leaving for tryouts.

"Well, Jackie, I didn't even know you played any baseball," said team trainer Harold Adanandus.

"Yeah," Jack responded. "I play a little."

THE NEGRO NATIONAL LEAGUE

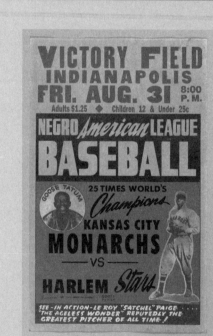

Negro League games often attracted more fans than Major League Baseball games.

In the 1880s, a few Black Americans, including Moses Fleetwood Walker and Bud Fowler, played professional baseball on otherwise all-white teams. By 1900, racist owners and players had forced all the Black players out of professional baseball. In response, Black Americans formed their own teams and played across the country. The most famous of these was the Chicago American Giants, owned by Andrew "Rube" Foster.

In February 1920, Foster met with the owners of seven other Black teams, and together they created the National Baseball League of the United States, known informally as the Negro National League (NNL). Foster served as president of the NNL, which included teams from Kansas City, Chicago, Cincinnati, Dayton, Detroit, Indianapolis, and St. Louis. In 1937, seven years after Foster's death, a new all-Black league formed—the Negro American League. This is the league that Jack played in during his season with the Kansas City Monarchs.

The leagues were successful in highlighting the professional abilities of Black players and attracting Black fans all over the United States. Jack's entry into Major League Baseball, in which he was followed by other Black stars joining MLB teams, contributed to the demise of the Negro American League.

The Monarchs were arguably the best team in the Negro Leagues. Their star-packed roster included pitcher Leroy "Satchel" Paige, whose fastball was famed and feared, and James "Cool Papa" Bell, the fastest base runner in professional ball.

Jack made the team without a problem. Both players and management knew that Jack had been an all-around star athlete at UCLA. He had struggled with baseball during the 1940 season at UCLA, but the Monarchs quickly saw that season as a fluke, not characteristic of his overall skills and abilities.

Jack was happy for the steady paycheck and the chance to learn from some of the greatest players in baseball history. But it didn't take long for him to feel that playing in the Negro Leagues was "a pretty miserable way to make a buck," as he later put it.

On his first day of spring training, he asked for his contract. Although a signed and dated contract was standard fare in many businesses, co-owner Baird refused to oblige, saying their prior exchange of letters was good enough. Jack wasn't pleased.

He also expected better management of the team schedule. But that wasn't on the owners' agenda, either. It rained on the second day of spring training, and the next day, the Monarchs played their first scheduled game—without having practiced together.

Then, during the regular season, a grinding schedule led Jack to complain about having to "jump between cities in uncomfortable buses and then play in games while half asleep and very tired."

The main problem was Jim Crow. There were no hotels for Black people in many of the places where they played, and if there were, the hotels were typically dingy, at least compared to nearby white ones.

"This fatiguing travel wouldn't have been so bad if we could have had decent meals," Jack remarked. But Jim Crow crushed that possibility, too. Most restaurants wouldn't serve Black people, and if there was a willing one, it usually offered only greasy takeout hamburgers.

The poor treatment rankled Jack, and sometimes he was so disgusted that he struck back.

Jack, bottom row, second from left, detested the Jim Crow conditions faced by the Kansas City Monarchs in 1945.

His teammates witnessed this firsthand when their bus stopped at a gas station in Oklahoma.

It had been a long trip up to this point, and Jack was already cranky as he got off the bus and walked toward the restroom.

"Boy, where are you going?" the white attendant called after him.

"I'm going to the restroom," Jack replied without breaking stride.

When the attendant told him for a second time to stay away from the restroom, Jack angrily demanded that he remove the gasoline hose from the tank. The Monarchs were not going to purchase fuel where they would not be allowed to use the restrooms.

Anxious to keep the sale, the frustrated attendant ultimately conceded. Jack used the bathroom, and the team proceeded on their way.

That bold act was a lesson for the team. The Monarchs had used this gas station many times before, but until this trip, no player had ever ventured to use the "whites only" restroom. Because of Jack's example, they now knew better.

Jack was equally impactful on the field.

He made dazzling plays at shortstop. He also boasted a .345 batting average and torched opponents with his lightning speed. His bunt play and base stealing were notorious.

The fans were not the only ones taking notice. One month into the Monarchs' regular season, Wendell Smith, a sportswriter for the *Pittsburgh Courier*, called on Jack for a special mission—to try out for the Boston Red Sox. Smith had learned that a Boston politician had successfully pressured the team to offer tryouts to Black players, and the sportswriter believed that Jack was one of the best candidates in the country.

Jack accepted the invitation, though he believed nothing would come of it, and on April 16, 1945, he and two other Black players, Sam Jethroe and Marvin Williams, fielded and batted balls at Fenway Park.

When Red Sox scout Hugh Duffy watched Jack, he reportedly said,

"What a ballplayer! Too bad he's the wrong color." Red Sox manager Eddie Collins agreed with Duffy. Although both found Jack's skills to be exceptional, they knew that Major League Baseball still followed the unwritten law that forbade teams from hiring Black players.

At the end of the tryout, Collins handed applications to each of the three players, saying that the Red Sox would be in touch with them.

No one called.

Jack played on. In just forty-seven games with the Monarchs, he managed to become one of the team's biggest draws.

Sportswriters were enamored. In June, a Delaware newspaper described Jack as the "Ace of [the] Monarchs," a "terrific slugger" with "uncanny skill at shortstop." The white writer pointed to Jack's third spot in the batting order on a team "studded with many outstanding players" as the best indication of his talent.

Bill Burk, a white sportswriter for the *Delaware County Daily Times*, described Jack's play in wider context. "The sensational infielder of the Monarchs is a colored boy," Burk wrote. "If he were white, the Lloyd Park [in Chester, Pennsylvania] would be filled two hours before game time with major league scouts, managers and owners, all trying to sign him up to a contract."

Red Sox Tryouts Given Trio of Colored Players

Manager Joe Cronin Watches Jethroe, Jackie Robinson, Marv Williams; Impressed, Report

BOSTON — Three promising members of colored professional baseball teams received short tryouts with the Boston Sox of the American League, here Monday. Working out under the watchful eyes of Manager Joe Cronin were Sam Jethroe of the Negro American Buckeyes, Jackie Robinson, shortstop of the Kansas City Monarchs (NAL), and Marvin Williams, promising young second baseman of the Philadelphia Stars.

Robinson is a former lieutenant in the Army with 31 months' service. He is an all-round athlete, having played all-American football as halfback at UCLA and nationally known as a basketball star. Cronin is said to have displayed keen interest in his performance.

It was an old insight. But this time, unknown to Burk, something new was afoot—a secret plan to offer Jack the elusive MLB contract.

Jack considered this "tryout" to be nothing more than a sham. (The *Afro-American*, April 28, 1945)

ELEVEN

STARING AT RICKEY

On August 24, 1945, Clyde Sukeforth found a spot near the visiting team's dugout at Comiskey Park in Chicago. Hometown fans had come to cheer for their beloved Giants, but the Brooklyn Dodger scout was there to watch rookie sensation Jack Robinson.

Sukeforth identified Jack by his number, 8, when the Kansas City Monarchs jogged onto the field for the pregame warm-up. "Hey, Robinson," he shouted. "I'm Clyde Sukeforth. I represent the Brooklyn Dodgers."

That got Jack's attention, and he strolled over to hear what the white man had to say. Sukeforth explained that Dodger manager Branch Rickey was starting a new ball club for Black players, the Brooklyn Brown Dodgers, and that he wanted to know about Jack's throwing abilities. So, could Jack throw to first base from "the hole," the far end of the shortstop position?

Jack shook his head, saying that he had a sore arm and wasn't scheduled to play for the next few days.

"I see," Sukeforth said. "But I sure would like to talk to you after the game."

Jack agreed and headed back to the field, where a teammate asked, "Who's the white fellow you were talking with?" When Jack said it was a scout from the Brooklyn Dodgers, they chuckled. The thought of

Dodger scout Clyde Sukeforth, shown here with Jack two years later, traveled to Chicago to check out Jack's throwing arm and to encourage him to meet with Dodger owner Branch Rickey.

a Major League Baseball scout at a Negro Leagues game was comical.

Jack later met up with Sukeforth at his hotel, and this time, their conversation dug deeper into Rickey's instructions and intentions.

"He told me to come out and see if you've got a shortstop's arm," Sukeforth explained again.

"Why is Mr. Rickey interested in my arm?" Jack pressed. "Why is he interested in *me*?"

Rickey hadn't given Sukeforth all the information he needed to answer Jack's question. His instructions were to check out Jack's arm, and if it was strong, to bring him to Brooklyn. Sukeforth mentioned that there was also something else.

"He *also* said that if you couldn't come to Brooklyn to see him, he would come to see you," Sukeforth said.

Both men understood the significance of that last point. Why would Rickey travel somewhere to meet a Black rookie for a Black team that didn't yet exist?

The more the two talked, the more they grew suspicious of Rickey's claim about launching the Brown Dodgers. "Jack, this could be the real thing," Sukeforth said, referring to the possibility of playing for the *Brooklyn* Dodgers.

Still, Jack was hesitant. He had been part of this song and dance before—when he had the sham tryout for the Boston Red Sox. Why would Brooklyn be any different?

But there was a difference, a major one. This time, Jack was not banging on anyone's door, trying to get inside a place that had barred him. This time, Rickey was banging on *his* door, inviting him to come to New York. Two days later, Jack made the journey by train, all expenses paid.

On the morning of August 28, Jack and Sukeforth walked into Rickey's office in Brooklyn. After brief introductions, Jack and Rickey sat quietly, sizing each other up for an uncomfortably long time.

"Oh, they were a pair, those two!" Sukeforth recalled. "I tell you, the air in that office was electric."

Finally, after quizzing Jack about his love life to find out if he would have a supportive partner at his side for the tough times ahead, Rickey turned to business. "You were brought here, Jackie, to play for the Brooklyn organization," he said. "Perhaps on Montreal to start with." The Montreal Royals were the top minor league team in the Dodger organization.

Rickey in the office where he and Jack met on August 28, 1945

Jack felt his stomach churning. As he remembered it, "I was thrilled, scared, and excited. I was incredulous. Most of all, I was speechless."

Rickey still had a lot to say. "I want to win the pennant and we need ballplayers!" he bellowed. "Do you think you can do it?"

Jack stared at Rickey, refusing to give him an immediate answer. As Sukeforth put it, "Jack waited, and waited, and waited before answering . . . We were all just looking at him."

In that tense moment, Jack held all the cards. He had the power to say yes. He had the power to say no. He had the power to stop Rickey. He had the power to undo Rickey's plan to desegregate Major League Baseball.

"Yes," Jack said.

WHY DID RICKEY CHOOSE JACK?

Some historians have argued that Jack was not the best player in the Negro Leagues when Branch Rickey chose him to join the Dodgers. Can you figure out which players might have been better? If there were better players, why did Rickey choose Jack instead of them? Some writers have suggested that Rickey settled on Jack not just because of his athletic skills but also because he was college-educated, a military veteran, and experienced in playing on integrated teams. What do you think?

Rickey was pleased, but he wasn't finished. He needed to address Jack's well-known temper.

"I know you're a good ballplayer," Rickey said. "What I don't know is whether you have the guts."

Jack could feel his cheeks getting hot. Ever since grade school, he had shown others that he was gutsy. Racist neighbors, Pasadena's police, opposing players, the US Army, the Negro Leagues—they all knew he had "guts."

Sensing Jack's anger, Rickey quickly backtracked and explained that it would take extraordinary courage because of what a Black player would face in MLB—beanballs, racist slurs, even physical attacks.

Jack's anger shifted into irritation. Was Rickey asking him to surrender his right to fight for his personal dignity? As he later put it, "I was twenty-six years old, and all my life back to the age of eight when a little neighbor girl called me a nigger—I had believed in payback, retaliation."

Staring at Rickey yet again, Jack asked, "Are you looking for a Negro who is afraid to fight back?"

This time, Rickey was hot. "Robinson," he said, "I'm looking for a ballplayer with guts enough not to fight back."

Rickey had a flair for drama, and in the next few minutes, he acted out the racist taunts, jeers, and attacks that Jack might face from players, coaches, and spectators. None of this was new to Jack. He had been a Black man in a racist world for a long time.

At the end of his role-playing, Rickey asked if Jack could withstand the racial animosity without "fighting back," without using violent words or actions.

Jack had been made for this moment. Although he believed in retaliation, he had long known that if he retaliated every time he faced a racist insult, he would have little energy for anything else. Plus, if he had constantly fought back, he would have been kicked out of school. He would have been ejected from every game. He would have received a dishonorable discharge from the army.

Jack had succeeded, especially in sports, because he had practiced selective retaliation. Rather than retaliating all the time, sometimes he had let others fight on his behalf. At other times, he had swallowed the insults and turned them into muscle and skills—the tools he used to vanquish his opponents on the football field, the baseball diamond, the basketball court, and the track field.

In those moments, the cause was to win a game or a tournament. But now, in this moment, the stakes were much higher. Would he swallow racist indignities for the cause of integrating Major League Baseball?

"I didn't know how I would do it," Jack recalled. "Yet I knew that I must. I had to do it for so many reasons. For black youth, for my mother, for Rae, for myself. I had already begun to feel I had to do it for Branch Rickey."

The battle was on.

The battle would be fought by Jack and Rachel, together. The couple had become engaged several years earlier and had experienced ups and downs along the way, including a breakup that left them not speaking to each other for a time.

During that period, Jack had even considered marrying another woman. But he eventually realized that Rachel "had more kindness, understanding and was more womanly than [anyone] I had ever known." The couple ironed out their differences and became engaged again.

On February 10, 1946, Reverend Karl Downs presided at their marriage at the Independent Church of Christ, the largest Black church in Los Angeles. Friends and family filled the sanctuary, and the couple was visibly nervous as they exchanged vows.

After the wedding, they checked into the Clark Hotel, the one Black hotel in the entire city. As Rachel recalled the moment, "It suddenly felt so right to be there, with Jack in that room, knowing we would now be together all the time, forever and ever. Really, when that door closed, I felt that all my troubles had melted away, and that a wonderful new life was beginning for Jack and for me."

Rachel decided to put her nursing career on hold. She had graduated with honors from UCLA's nursing program, and she had worked as a nurse in New York City. But now she would use her education, training, and experience for wounds outside the hospital.

TWELVE

CRUSHING
THE MINORS

Montreal manager Clay Hopper, center, speaks with Jack and shortstop Stanley Breard at Roosevelt Stadium in Jersey City, New Jersey, on opening day, April 18, 1946.

C lutching her handbag, Rachel slowly made her way through a boisterous crowd of revelers at Roosevelt Stadium in Jersey City, New Jersey. It was April 18, 1946, opening day for the Jersey City Giants, always an unofficial holiday. It was also Jack's minor league debut with the Montreal Royals, and that attracted national attention.

Rachel tried to scan the field for her husband, but the massive crowd made it difficult for her to see anything other than a sea of bodies. Mayor Frank Hague had closed schools for the day, and ticket sales had skyrocketed to 51,872, more than double the park's official capacity.

As she settled into her seat, Rachel felt anxious and concerned. Her shakiness stemmed from the vicious racism that she and Jack had encountered at spring training in Florida. "It was kind of horrendous with all the raw racial attacks," she recalled.

In the town of Sanford, Florida, a white mob had planned to march on the home where they were staying. Branch Rickey found out about the planned attack and instructed Jack and Rachel to leave immediately and head to nearby Daytona Beach. But the threats and indignities of Jim Crow ruled their lives there, too, even at the ballpark, where Rachel had to sit in a segregated area.

Would anything be different in the North, in New Jersey, on opening day?

Jersey City Giants fans spewed every racial slur imaginable when Jack took the field. At first Rachel cringed, but then she noticed a powerful chorus of cheers from Black fans who had traveled from as far away as Baltimore to watch Jack make history. That brightened her outlook, but only a bit.

Jack's heart raced as the brass band performed the national anthem. His stomach, he said, felt "as if it were full of feverish fireflies with claws on their feet."

As much as he worried about the spectators, he also wondered about the support of his team, including manager Clay Hopper, whom Canadian sportswriter Austin "Dink" Carroll once described as "a Southern gentleman of the old school." When Branch Rickey had first told Hopper about Jack, the Montreal manager said, "Do you really think a nigger's a human being?"

Jack felt the enormity of the moment during his first at bat. Photographers swarmed behind home plate, and all eyes were focused on him. His knees felt rubbery, and his palms were almost "too moist to grip the bat."

Nerves got the better of him. On a full count from pitcher Warren Sandel, Jack grounded out to the shortstop. While his fans let out a big sigh of disappointment, his detractors sneered and snorted.

In the third inning, when the Royals were leading by two and his pregame jitters were under control, Jack strode to home plate, ready to show what he was made of.

With Sandel still on the mound and two runners on base, Jack connected on a fastball. His fans leaped to their feet, trying to track the screaming ball. Some pointed toward left field, some put their hands to their mouths, some just gawked. Before anyone could say "Jack Robinson," the ball whizzed over the left-field fence.

Gone!

His fans erupted. They punched their fists into the air, they hugged one another, they danced in the aisles.

Montreal teammate George Shuba shakes Jack's hand after he crushed a three-run homer on opening day in 1946.

Jack began his victory trot around the bases. With the pressure off, he couldn't contain his smile. Clay Hopper, standing between third and home, offered his new star player a congratulatory pat on the back.

At home plate, George Shuba, the next batter in the lineup, quickly weighed what to do. Like Hopper, Shuba was from the Deep South. Shaking the hand of a Black man would surely be frowned upon in his hometown of Mobile, Alabama.

Shuba extended his hand, and Jack took it. Together, in that brief public exchange, they defied more than fifty years of Jim Crow.

Opening Day Throng Cheers Jackie's Homer; Montreal Wins 2, Loses 2

Royal Second Baseman Individual Star of Inaugural, Hits Safely in Four Straight

NEWARK—Though by no means as sensational as he was in his debut at Jersey City on Thursday when 30,000 patrons saw him steal the opening day show from Mayor Frank Hague and the more celebrated stars of the International League, Jackie Robinson continued his brilliant performance for the Montreal Royals on Saturday at Jersey City and on Sunday here.

The fact of the matter is that the scintillating Montreal Royal second baseman could hardly be expected to continue his opening day pace when he turned in a day's effort of:

(1) Blasting a home-run with two men on base;
(2) Getting four hits in five times at bat;
(3) Knocking in four runs;
(4) Scoring four runs himself;
(5) Stealing two bases;
(6) Tricking opposing pitchers into making two balks;
(7) Starting the only Montreal double-play, and
(8) Handling six chances with but one error.

With news photographers milling around home plate in general confusion, Robinson's first turn at bat resulted in a scorching grounder to shortstop off Southpaw Pitcher Warren Sandel, just sent here from the New York Giants.

by George Shuba.

He was put out on his first official trip to the plate in the third inning on a slow infield roller.

He reached first base on his second official time at bat with a single, and after advancing to second base on a steal, crossed the plate for his second run of the game when Red Durett hit out of the park for a homer.

Robinson drew a walk in the ninth inning and was caught attempting to steal, the first time he had been caught in five such chances.

The Royals swept the Jersey City series 14-1 and 9-1.

On Sunday, however, they did not fare so well, dropping both ends of the bargain bill, 1-0 and 7-6.

Sunday's matinee affair saw Robbie handling six chances afield with one bobble. He was given a rest in the nightcap when no Newark batters hit in his direction.

The Royals play here Monday and Tuesday, move to Syracuse for games Wednesday, Thursday and Friday, and thence to Baltimore to engage the Orioles, Saturday, Sunday and Monday.

Robbie Bats .533 for First Week's Games

NEWARK, N.J.—Jackie Robinson, Montreal Royal second baseman, had connected for 8 hits in 15 times at bat at the close of Sunday's doubleheader in Newark, thus completing his first week in organized baseball with a respectable .533 average.

	AB.	R.	H.
Thursday	5	4	4
Saturday	2	2	1
Sunday	8	1	3
	—	—	—
Totals	15	7	8
Percentage			.533

Under intense pressure, Jack performed well on opening day (*The Afro-American,* April 27, 1946)

"Hell," Shuba later said, "he was on our side, wasn't he? No problem."

One anxious admirer was finally able to lean back in her seat. Jack's spectacular home run, coupled with the ecstatic cheers, had eased Rachel's fears.

But her husband was far from done. In his five at bats, Jack belted four hits, scored four runs, and stole two bases, leading the Royals to a crushing 14–1 victory over the Giants.

After the game, well-wishers clogged the Montreal locker room to congratulate Jack on his outstanding performance. It was a "mad scene" according to one witness. Another said Jack was as "happy as a kid on Christmas morning."

Beaming, he shook hands, chatted with reporters, and lavished praise on his teammates.

"The one thing that I cared about was the way my teammates backed me up all the way," he explained. "There wasn't any riding out there but if there was, I wouldn't have minded as long as my team was behind me. They have been swell."

Back home later, Rachel breathed a sigh of relief. Seeing the fans reveling in Jack's dazzling performance had temporarily relieved her worry. But she also took a deep breath, knowing that there would be obstacles ahead. And she was right. In the coming days, hostile fans sought to derail Jack's season.

On the team's first trip to Baltimore, the southernmost city on their schedule, Branch Rickey learned of the possibility that a violent mob would target Jack. Although no physical violence took place, the abuse that Jack received there was so vicious that Rachel cried in their hotel room. "She wanted me to quit," he recalled.

Jack understood her reaction, but he had been prepared for the

Jack's base stealing helped to shatter attendance records during his stint with Montreal.

vitriol and hostility. There was nothing he heard from the Baltimore fans that he hadn't heard when playing football for UCLA.

The indignities were not limited to time spent in the South, either. Jack also faced a harsh reception in upstate New York.

"Syracuse rode me harder than any other city in the circuit," he remembered. "They were tough on me both on the field and in the stands."

Garton Del Savio, second baseman for the Syracuse Chiefs, recalled his teammates calling Jack "some of the foulest names he'd ever heard, the 'worst things' you can scream at another man." Some Syracuse players had even arrived for the game in blackface.

Still, Baltimore gave Syracuse stiff competition for having the meanest fans. Later in the season, on June 7, Baltimore fans stormed the field on the final out, loudly threatening to assault Jack, who had already retreated to the clubhouse. Hurling racist words, they remained in the park until one in the morning. Several of Jack's teammates stayed with him in the locker room until the mob finally dissipated.

CRUSHING THE MINORS   89

Through it all, Jack remained stalwart. More important, he did not retaliate, except by performing at the highest level and helping his team win game after game.

In an action-packed season that saw the Royals compile an impressive 100–54 record, Jack led the league in batting, posting a .349 batting average. He also led in runs with 113 and finished second in stolen bases with 40.

The Royals easily captured the pennant, and Jack and his teammates capped off their extraordinary play with a six-game victory over the Louisville Colonels in the Junior World Series.

Jack's teammates marveled at his performance and his composure.

"Most of us could not comprehend that he was able to perform so magnificently under such tremendous pressure," George Shuba said.

By then, it was clear to everyone, including Clay Hopper, that Branch Rickey had been right—Jack Robinson had the talent to play in the majors.

At the end of the season, the Montreal skipper acknowledged not only Jack's playing ability but also his impeccable character. "He's a big-league ballplayer, a good team hustler, and a real gentleman," Hopper said.

Jack's successful season was a powerful affirmation of his unwavering self-confidence and ability to overcome adversity. One question remained: Could he also succeed in the majors?

Checking out his competition on opening day in 1947

THIRTEEN

BECOMING
JACKIE AGAIN

J ust before the start of the 1947 season, the Brooklyn Dodgers
announced that Jack would join the team on opening day. The
historic news came in the form of a simple written statement distributed to the media on April 10: "The Brooklyn Dodgers today
purchased the contract of Jackie Roosevelt Robinson from the Montreal Royals."

Jack was elated. The chance to make history in a Dodger uniform
was thrilling beyond measure. "I know now that dreams do come
true," he said.

His teammates did not share the dream.

During spring training, right fielder Dixie Walker, a native of Birmingham, Alabama, had tried to rally the team to make sure that Jack
would not appear on the roster. As a traditional white Southerner,
Walker believed in white supremacy and racial segregation. At least
several other Dodgers, from the South and the North, openly backed
his campaign.

Brooklyn manager Leo Durocher blew his stack when he learned
of the clubhouse revolt. "I don't care if the guy is yellow or black, or if
he has stripes like a [expletive] zebra," he yelled at the white players.
"I'm the manager of this team, and I say he plays."

W. E. B. DU BOIS AND BLACK DOUBLE-CONSCIOUSNESS

W. E. B. Du Bois in 1918

In 1897, African American scholar W. E. B. Du Bois published a now-famous article titled "Strivings of the Negro People." The article introduced the concept of "double-consciousness," or "twoness."

According to Du Bois, "double-consciousness" refers partly to Black people's awareness that white people hold them in contempt merely because of the color of their skin. "It is a peculiar sensation, this double-consciousness, this sense of always looking at one's self through the eyes of others, of measuring one's soul by the tape of a world that looks on in amused contempt and pity," Du Bois wrote. "One ever feels his two-ness. An American, a Negro; two souls, two thoughts, two unreconciled strivings; two warring ideals in one dark body, whose dogged strength alone keeps it from being torn asunder."

On opening day, April 15, 1947, Brooklyn fans greeted Walker with a chorus of boos. The right fielder must have been shocked, because up to this point, fans had fondly referred to him as "People's Choice."

But times had changed. On this opening day, unlike all the earlier ones, about three-fifths of the fans in attendance were Black people.

Walker's fan base, by contrast, consisted mostly of white Brooklynites, and many of them had stayed home for the season opener. Perhaps they were unwilling to rub shoulders with Black fans, or to see a Black man in a Dodger uniform, or both.

Whatever the case, Black fans had turned out in droves, and because they knew of Walker's opposition to Jack, they gave him an earful. Dixie Walker was *not* the "Black People's Choice."

The Brooklyn Dodgers' new first baseman, Jack Robinson, was.

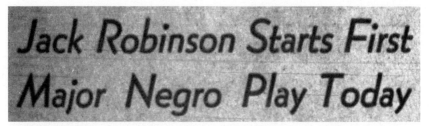

The Elizabethton Star *in Tennessee was one of the few newspapers to use "Jack" in its main article about his debut on April 15, 1947.*

When Jack jogged out to take his position on the field at the top of the first inning, Black fans were euphoric. The historic moment was not only his dream come alive, it was theirs, too. They clapped and cheered. They smiled and waved. They slapped one another on the back and thrust their fists into the air.

Rachel beamed from her seat behind the Dodger dugout. Cradled in her arms was the newest member of the Robinson family—Jackie Jr., or, as his parents called him, "Sugar Lump."

Like all the fans around her, Rachel realized the significance of Jack's unmistakable presence on the diamond. Never again would Major League Baseball be a lily-white sport. Some people said that the country would never be the same.

WAS JACK THE FIRST?

Moses Fleetwood Walker played catcher for the Toledo Blue Stockings in 1884.

"The first to play major league baseball openly as a black man" was Moses Fleetwood Walker, according to John R. Husman, writing for the Society for American Baseball Research. Richard Goldstein of the *New York Times* agrees: "Moses Fleetwood Walker remains the first major leaguer recognized in his time as an African-American." In ESPN's *The Undefeated*, John Harris also describes Walker as "the first African-American to play professional baseball." If this is true, why is Jack Robinson credited as being the first Black player in Major League Baseball when he debuted with the Brooklyn Dodgers on April 15, 1947? How should we describe Jack? As the second Black player in Major League Baseball? As the first Black player in Major League Baseball in the twentieth century?

Jack was pleased that Black fans were on his side, and that some white Brooklynites would give him a fair chance, but he still felt a bit uneasy and tense. It was a strange feeling. It was as if he was a Dodger and yet not a Dodger.

That feeling had taken root a few days earlier when he first entered the Dodger locker room. "I looked for a locker with 'Jackie Robinson' on it, but couldn't find one," he recalled. "In fact, there were lockers for everyone but me."

Most of his teammates ignored him as he stood there. A few shook his hand and welcomed him to the team, but the great majority simply turned away, laughing and joking among themselves.

Shut out of their white Dodger world, Jack could not help but feel different from everyone else—*on* the team but not *part* of the team.

The clubhouse manager gave him his uniform and asked him to use a folding chair near the back of the room. As Jack recalled the scene, "I finally got dressed and looked at myself in the mirror. I was wearing a brand-new uniform—No. 42. It fit me and was comfortable, but I still felt like a stranger, or an uninvited guest."

Making matters worse, Jack felt obliged to be an *acceptable* guest.

To succeed as a Dodger, he understood that he would have to continue to tamp down the part of himself that was a relentless and uncompromising Black freedom fighter.

He would have to be "Jackie," a nonthreatening Black man who would be acceptable to the Dodgers, Major League Baseball, and the country.

As "Jackie," Jack would have to be poised and patient, nonviolent in the face of violence, and quiet in response to racist rants. As if that wasn't tough enough, he was also required to be a wild (but tamed) success on the diamond.

Jack had been "Jackie" before, in the minor leagues, but now he would have to be "Jackie" on the biggest stage of "America's favorite pastime."

_____

Perhaps it was the sense that he was a Dodger and yet not a Dodger that caused him to go hitless in his first two at bats. Perhaps it was the inner struggle to be both "Jack" and "Jackie." Maybe it was just a case of nervousness.

But none of that ultimately mattered. Jack bunted on his third trip to the plate, and he scored a run that helped the Dodgers beat the Boston Braves 5–3.

As he left the stadium for home, about 250 fans swarmed around him. "Jackie!" they shouted, trying to shake his hand and pat his back. Some wanted his autograph on their baseballs, and he obliged, signing them "Jackie Robinson."

Most members of the friendly mob were white people. If Jack was surprised, he soon understood that if he could help the Dodgers win the pennant, he was *their* man, too.

FOURTEEN

CONTROLLING
HIS TEMPER

I n his first few days with the Dodgers, Jack reveled in the warm reception that fans gave him at Ebbets Field. There were minor incidents, including the predictable racial slurs, but for the most part, the nastiness that Branch Rickey had forecast was refreshingly absent.

That changed on the frigid afternoon of April 22, 1947, when the Philadelphia Phillies arrived to battle the Dodgers. A torrent of abuse drenched Jack as soon as he walked toward home plate for his first at bat.

"Hey, nigger," someone shouted, "why don't you go back to the cotton field where you belong?"

"They're waiting for you in the jungles, black boy!"

Jack immediately realized that the vicious insults were coming from the Phillies dugout, and that the loudest voice belonged to manager Ben Chapman.

"We don't want you here, nigger!" they yelled.

"Go back to the bushes!"

Jack had heard racist insults throughout his life, but these felt unrelenting and intensely personal. Plus, they were coming from a northern team on Dodger territory. Were there no safe spaces anywhere?

The assaults continued as Chapman and his cohorts shouted that Jack had fat lips, a thick skull, and infectious sores and diseases.

WHY DID JACK USE THE NAME "JACKIE"?

Jack signed his name as "Jack" in high school, college, and the army. He also used "Jack" when signing baseballs during his stint with the Montreal Royals. But in 1947, after he debuted with the Brooklyn Dodgers, he typically used "Jackie" when signing baseballs, letters, and cards. Why did he make the change?

Note the progression of signatures on these signed baseballs. The "Jack Robinson" signature on the left comes from his 1936 season at John Muir Technical High School. The other "Jack Robinson," middle, is from his 1946 season with the Montreal Royals. And the "Jackie Robinson" signature is from his 1947 season with the Brooklyn Dodgers.

The Dodgers sat by silently. They knew that Branch Rickey had instructed him not to retaliate, and yet they did not defend him.

Jack simmered with rage. "I was, after all, a human being," he later said.

He also wanted to smash some white teeth. As he put it, "For one wild and rage-crazed moment I thought, 'To hell with Mr. Rickey's "noble experiment." ... To hell with the image of the patient black freak I was supposed to create. I would throw down my bat, stride over to the Phillies dugout, grab one of those white sons of bitches and smash his teeth in with my despised black fist.'"

But Jack swallowed hard and composed himself. The stakes were much bigger than the momentary pleasure of pummeling Chapman and his puppets.

Despite making his first error in the majors, Jack had a solid game. He singled, took third base on an error, and touched home plate after a hit from Gene Hermanski. It was the game's only score.

Jack felt alone in his struggles. But that, too, changed, at least a bit, when the Phillies reignited their racist onslaught in the second of the three-game series.

According to Jack's later account, Dodger second baseman Ed Stanky berated Chapman and his team. "Listen, you yellow-bellied cowards," he reportedly said, "why don't you yell at somebody who can answer back?"

Still, most of the Dodgers sat on their hands and kept their mouths shut, leaving their teammate to simmer in silence.

But fans came to his defense. After witnessing Chapman's brutish behavior, they wrote letters of complaint to MLB commissioner Happy Chandler. In turn, Chandler warned the Phillies that if they continued to harass Jack, they would face punishment. Worried about his job, Chapman agreed to stop his assaults.

Strike Against Jackie Spiked

Rickey Terms Rumor 'Tempest in Teapot'
By SAM LACY
AFRO Sports Editor

PHILADELPHIA

Despite emphatic denials on the part of principal characters in the drama, it is an established fact that a move to promote a strike against the presence of Jackie Robinson in the National League was on foot here and in Brooklyn last week.

The strike, instigated by a small bloc of St. Louis Cardinal players who had fantastic visions of a general walkout later, was checked by League President Ford Frick and Cardinal owner Sam Breadon. Both denied this, however.

Although some players talked of using a strike to force Jack out of MLB, no strike ever took place. (The Afro-American, May 17, 1947)

In May, the Dodgers traveled to Philadelphia for their second series with the Phillies.

The stay in the "City of Brotherly Love" got off to a horrible start when Harold Parrott, the Dodgers' travel arranger, discovered that the Benjamin Franklin Hotel would not allow the team to sleep there.

"And don't bring your team back here while you have any Nigras with you!" the hotel manager told Parrott.

Rather than showing support for Jack, Parrott arranged for him to stay at an all-Black hotel. With Jack off the guest list, the Ben Franklin manager welcomed the rest of the team to the swanky hotel. No one protested the injustice.

Jack suffered another indignity the following night when Phillies manager Ben Chapman asked to be photographed with him. Chapman was worried that Jack's fans might turn violent, and he thought that a friendly photograph would help calm the volatile situation.

Although Jack no doubt winced at the request, he obliged and smiled for the camera. He later said that "having my picture taken with this man was one of the most difficult things I had to make myself do."

During the awkward photo session, Chapman reportedly said: "Jackie, you know, you're a good ballplayer, but you're still a nigger to me."

Jack found it difficult to pose for this photo with Ben Chapman, the bigoted manager of the Philadelphia Phillies, on May 10, 1947.

Jack's encounters with the Phillies were just some of the indignities

'Get Out Of Baseball,' Poison Pen Letters Warn Robinson

In an effort to track down the source of the poison pen letters police assigned a special detail to the case. One detective was sent out of town to trace the signer of the "Get out of baseball!" letter but found the name and address to be fictitious.

"A police captain came to my house this morning," said Robinson, a former Army lieutenant, "and asked about the letters. I told him that if I got any, I wouldn't be turning them over to the police but would take it up with the Brooklyn club."

POLICE ESCORT

Observed leaving the ball park each day with a two-man police escort, Jackie was asked whether he had received any threats. Apparently regarding the notes as "crank letters" Jackie shook his head and said, "The cops are just to keep the autograph hounds from mobbing me."

Jack received a police escort after an investigation into letters threatening his life. (New Journal and Guide, May 17, 1947)

that he endured in his first season. He and Rachel also faced numerous death threats, and at least one person threatened to kidnap Jackie Jr. On the field, Jack was hit by more pitches than any other player in the early part of the season.

The struggle was Jack's alone to bear. It wasn't Major League Baseball's. It wasn't his teammates'. It wasn't even Branch Rickey's. It was Jack alone who swallowed the insults, and it was Jack alone who once again turned the insults into energy and muscle.

At the end of the regular season, he led his team in singles, successful bunts, stolen bases, and runs scored. *Sporting News* named him Rookie of the Year. Perhaps no other Dodger had contributed to the team's success more than he had. Once again, Jack was a superstar.

The Dodgers lost to the Yankees in the 1947 World Series, but Jack had won the respect of many of his teammates. And his intelligence, strength, and courage had inspired countless Black people, especially children and teens, to fight racism in their own lives. More than a Dodger superstar, Jack was their favorite activist—their personal hero in their own fight for Black freedom.

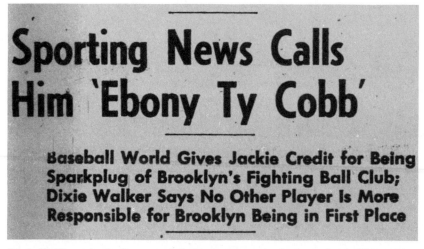

Sporting News Calls Him 'Ebony Ty Cobb'

Baseball World Gives Jackie Credit for Being Sparkplug of Brooklyn's Fighting Ball Club; Dixie Walker Says No Other Player Is More Responsible for Brooklyn Being in First Place

Dixie Walker, who had opposed Jack's presence on the team, lauded his perfor-mance near the end of the 1947 season, when Sporting News *named Jack Rookie of the Year. (Pittsburgh Courier, September 20, 1947)*

FIFTEEN

STRAIGHTENING HIS BACK

J ack glanced at his prepared comments. His light-colored suit, illuminated by camera flashes, highlighted his broad shoulders. Rachel, wearing an elegant dark dress, sat next to him.

Although he had often made public statements, this one was different. On this day, July 18, 1949, his audience was a special committee of the US Congress.

The main purpose of the House Un-American Activities Committee (HUAC) was to investigate citizens suspected of having ties to communism and to the Soviet Union, the most powerful communist country in the world.

Jack was not a suspect. He was an invited guest, and his role was to deliver damning testimony against a popular Black man.

Paul Robeson, shown in an undated photograph, spoke at the Soviet Union–sponsored World Peace Conference in Paris, April 1949

In the summer of 1949, HUAC was investigating the question of whether African Americans were loyal to the United States. Committee members believed that Soviet-friendly communists had infiltrated Black civil rights groups.

HUAC focused its attention on Paul Robeson, a famous Black entertainer and civil rights activist. Robeson had run afoul of the committee in April, after delivering a speech in Paris to a group called the World Congress of the Partisans of Peace.

According to a news report, Robeson said that it was "unthinkable that American Negroes would go to war on behalf of those who have oppressed us for generations against the Soviet Union which in one generation has raised our people to the full dignity of mankind."

Just after the report was published, Robeson claimed that he had never spoken those words, and while his rebuttal was accurate, his reputation had already been badly damaged.

HUAC saw Robeson as a traitor and invited Jack to denounce him in a congressional hearing.

Jack seemed to be a safe if not ideal choice. He was a Black man opposed to communism. He was the symbol of a gradual approach to limited integration. He was also at least as popular as Robeson. In the 1949 season, he led the National League in batting and had received more votes for MLB's All-Star Game than any other player in the league.

But Jack was wary of accepting the invitation. HUAC had a reputation for destroying the careers of those it targeted, and Jack wanted no part in that.

He also had little interest in criticizing Robeson in public. As he put it later, "Rae and I remembered how, as children, we had thrilled to Robeson's success, had hummed the tunes made famous by his booming bass-baritone voice." The couple also deeply respected Robeson for his longtime fight against Jim Crow.

But Jack wanted to make sure that white racists could not point to so-called "Negro disloyalty" as a reason for stopping the advance of civil rights. Black Americans had fought in every major war, and he believed that most would continue to be red-blooded patriots.

Wavering, Jack talked with Rachel, who encouraged him to follow his instincts, and with Branch Rickey, who said that Jack's testimony before Congress would help advance racial integration in Major League Baseball and across the United States.

Friends and strangers also weighed in. Some said that if he appeared before HUAC, he would be a "traitor," an "Uncle Tom" more interested in pleasing white people than in fighting for Black rights.

Jack accepted the invitation.

COMMUNISM

Communism called for abolishing private property; Jack believed in an individual's right to own property. Soviet communism seized private businesses for government control; Jack believed in an individual's right to own and operate a business. Communism denounced belief in God; Jack was a Christian. Soviet communism denied the right to worship; Jack believed in an individual's right to worship freely.

The congressional room was hot, stuffy, and jam-packed, but Jack appeared cool, calm, and collected as he began to read his statement.

In a cordial tone, he announced that he was "an expert on being a colored American, with thirty years of experience at it."

As expected, he also commented on Robeson's statement. But to the committee's surprise, his response was short, even terse: "I haven't

The New York Age *reported that Black Harlemites were divided over the question of whether Jack should have testified against Paul Robeson.*

any comment to make, except that the statement, if Mr. Robeson actually made it, sounds very silly to me."

Jack conceded that some Black Americans were indeed communists and would choose not to fight against Russia. But, he added, "most Negroes ... would do their best to help their country win the war—against Russia, or any other enemy that threatened us."

Then, in what must have been a shock to committee members, Jack defended Robeson's constitutional right to free speech. Robeson, he said, "has a right to his personal views, and if he wants to sound silly when he expresses them in public, that's his business and not mine. He's still a famous athlete and a great singer and actor."

Jack also criticized HUAC members, without mentioning them, for investigating Black loyalty to the United States. The only people who ever questioned "my race's loyalty," he said, were "a few people who don't add to much."

Digging deeper, Jack also faulted the committee for failing to see that racial discrimination was at least as threatening to democracy as communism was.

"White people must realize that the more a Negro hates communism because it opposes democracy, the more he is going to hate any other influence that kills off democracy in this country—and that goes for racial discrimination in the Army, and segregation on trains and buses, and job discrimination because of religious beliefs or color or place of birth."

Digging still deeper, Jack even suggested that racial discrimination was a far more fundamental problem than communism. "Negroes were stirred up long before there was a Communist Party," he claimed, "and they'll stay stirred up long after the party has disappeared—unless Jim Crow has disappeared by then as well."

HUAC's members, especially the Southern segregationists, were angry at Jack's sharp words about their support for Jim Crow. But what could they do? They had invited him, and he had turned on them. Scrambling for cover, they ignored Jack's attacks on racial discrimination and focused on his short critique of Robeson. The white media did the same.

In contrast, some members of the Black media downplayed Jack's comment about Robeson and highlighted his takedown of Jim Crow. One headline in a Black newspaper read, "Jackie Flays Bias in Army."

In August, about a month after Jack's testimony, white veterans in Peekskill, New York, formed a mob and attacked a civil rights concert where Robeson was slated to perform. The mob destroyed the stage, burned crosses and an effigy of Robeson, and beat concertgoers.

Jack was angry when he read an article about the assault.

"Paul Robeson should have the right to sing, speak, or do anything he wants to," he said. "Those mobs make it tough on everyone . . . They say here in America you're allowed to be whatever you want. I think those rioters ought to be investigated."

Jack's comments about Robeson, during and after his HUAC

appearance, marked an important turning point in his fight for justice. Up to this point in his baseball career, he had been largely quiet about the injustices he faced on the field and about those that Black Americans confronted everywhere. He had been "Jackie," determined to be the person who would be acceptable to Major League Baseball—and to America.

But now, Jack was a loud critic of Jim Crow, a public spokesman for Black freedom.

Fans also noticed that he was becoming much more assertive on the diamond, arguing against calls that he found unfair. Sportswriters who penned unflattering articles also experienced his wrath.

It seemed that Jack was freeing himself from the requirement to be "Jackie," the acceptable guest in MLB, and that he was returning to "Jack," the uncompromising Black freedom fighter.

All the while, he continued to excel on the playing field. By the end of the 1949 season, he batted .342 and led MLB in stolen bases. A committee of the Baseball Writers' Association of America named him the Most Valuable Player in the National League. Still, the abuse continued.

SIXTEEN

KICKING JACKIE

J ack fumed as he dug his foot into the batter's box. It wasn't a bad call that made him angry. Nor was it a beanball. It was a sarcastic heckle from former Dodger manager Leo Durocher, now skipper for the New York Giants. Jack and Durocher had a strained relationship by this point. Durocher had supported Jack's entry into MLB, but at the beginning of the 1948 season, he had publicly humiliated Jack, in front of his teammates and reporters, for putting on weight. Durocher's vicious words still stung. Making matters worse, the two men were now on opposing teams that despised each other.

"Get the manager out of there!" Durocher had yelled to his pitcher.

Like others, the Giants manager had heard rumors that Jack was trying to exert his authority in the clubhouse and determine the team's direction.

The snarky comment was still stinging when Jack later took his position at second base and saw Durocher standing in the first-base coaching box.

"Are you wearing your wife's perfume tonight, Leo?" Jack yelled.

The manager was accustomed to ribbings about how much cologne he used, but he could not abide by Jack's reference to his wife, Laraine.

Durocher fired back, asking Jack if he wanted "to get personal."

"You're damned right I do, if you do," Jack replied.

"You've got a swelled head!" Durocher shouted, using his arms to show what he meant.

War Declaration

Irvin Homers

NEW YORK (NNPA) — Monty Irvin, New York Giants outfielder, got a solo home run in the fourth inning of the game in which the New York Giants defeated the Boston Braves, Saturday, 4-2. At bat five times, he also was credited with a single.

Hank Thompson, the Giants' third baseman, was credited with two hits in four trips.

Sam Jethroe, the Braves' speedy centerfielder, got one hit in five tries.

Irvin was credited with three hits, including two doubles, in five times at bat as the Braves rallied in the ninth inning last Friday night to defeat the Giants, 8 to 4

Dodgers Sign 2 More Tan Stars

Bob Wilson, Jim Wilks
Bought from Houston

NEW YORK (ANP) — The Brooklyn Dodgers have purchased the contracts of two outfielders of the Houston Eagles of the Negro American League, Bob Wilson and James E. Wlks.

Both have been assigned to the Elmira, N.Y., team of the Eastern League.

In 30 games this season Wilson was batting .357 with 45 hits in 126 trips to the plate. In 1949 he ranked eighth in the league in batting with a mark of .355, on 93 hits in 262 times at bat in 60 games for the Eagles.

Wilks, in 31 games, hits safely only 27 times in 127 times at bat, for an average of .213. Last year he batted .257 with 67 hits in 261 trips to the plate. His 12 stolen bases ranked him fourth in that department.

Wilks was in a three-way tie for second place in fielding among outfielders last season with a mark of .978. He committed only four errors out of 186 chances.

Leo Durocher, New York Giants manager (lower right) makes with the "swelled head" gesture at Jackie Robinson as the two step up the tempo in their long-time feud. Action occurred at Ebbets Field last week at the height of a heated exchange between the Dodger second baseman and his former manager.

A dramatic moment in the feud between Jack and his former manager Leo Durocher, who makes a "swelled head" gesture at Jack from the first base coach's box (Afro-American, July 8, 1950)

The fiery exchange on June 28, 1950, revealed not only the contempt that Jack and Durocher had for each other. It also showed that Jack was no longer the quiet and unassertive player of past years.

"Fans Like the New Jackie Robinson; So Does B. Rickey" read a headline not long after the public feud. The headline appeared in the *Los Angeles Sentinel*, an esteemed Black newspaper, topping an article about changes in Jack's persona.

"Robinson started out as a brooding, patient, poker-faced big league rookie in 1947," the article stated. But recently, he "has taken on a forceful, daring and outspoken aggressiveness."

Jack's transformation pleased not only his fans but also the man who, back in 1946, had asked him to "turn the other cheek."

"Robinson is showing what we knew he had in him the whole time," Branch Rickey said. "In fact, his aggressive nature was the biggest worry we had. His greatest job has been in keeping it under control until circumstances permitted him to show his true ability."

A week after his battle with Durocher, Jack got into another argument, this one with an umpire.

Jack was in the middle of an impressive streak when he came to bat in the second inning of a game against the Phillies. He had hit successfully in the last sixteen games, and he had made it to base in the last fifty-five.

The streak came to an ignoble end shortly after he struck out on a called third strike. Jack was not happy with the call, and he shook his head.

"That pitch was right down the middle," said umpire Jocko Conlan.

"My ass," Jack angrily replied.

Conlan promptly threw him out of the game.

Enraged, Jack launched into a verbal tirade against the umpire. He was so angry that Dodger coach Clyde Sukeforth had to restrain him and escort him back to the dugout.

After the game, Jack accused Conlan of "goading" him.

"What does he have to say that for?" Jack told the media. "It's bad enough to be called out on strikes, but to have an umpire criticize you for it, that's going too far."

Five days later, he was ejected again. Umpire Lou Jorda heard players harassing him from the dugout, suspected Jack, and tossed him from the game.

In response, Jack tore onto the field and protested that he hadn't said a word. Once again, Sukeforth had to hold him back.

Jorda reportedly conceded that he "might have put out the wrong guy."

This incident, coupled with others, led Jack to complain that umpires were targeting him unfairly.

"There's no question in my mind that umpires are picking on Robinson," Sukeforth added.

Dodger manager Burt Shotton went further, suggesting that the umpires targeted Jack because he was a Black man. "You can bet that if Robinson were somebody else, no umpire would pay any attention to it."

Jack said the same thing. He also continued to stand up for himself when he felt that others had wronged him.

On July 17, 1952, he blew a major gasket in a game against the Cincinnati Reds at Crosley Field.

In the ninth inning, with the Dodgers ahead by a run, the Reds'

Kicked in the air during the July 17, 1952, altercation, Jack's glove appears just above the home run fence in the upper righthand corner.

Ed Pellagrini attempted a steal. Jack tagged him as he slid hard into second.

"Safe," yelled the umpire.

Jack went ballistic. He screamed. He jumped up and down. He slammed the ball and his glove into the ground. He screamed some more. And then he picked up his glove and booted it about twenty feet into the air. It was a strong, glorious kick, reminiscent of his days as a kicker for PJC and UCLA.

Jack was kicked out of the game — and fined fifty dollars.

In a later interview, he said: "I know it's wrong for me to lose my temper. It doesn't do me any good and I really make an effort not to do it. The wife is after me about it all the time, too."

Jack also commented about the widely published photograph of him kicking his glove.

"I hate to see things like that," he said. "I could prevent them by curbing my temper, but when an umpire makes an obvious mistake, it seems I automatically blow up. I just can't help myself."

At the same time, Jack acknowledged that he could indeed help himself. After all, he had curbed his temper from 1946 to 1948.

"No promises," he said, "but I'll try."

Perhaps the most significant time he lost his temper occurred near the end of his playing days, in a game against the Milwaukee Braves.

In the top of the second inning, pitcher Lew Burdette, who was not in the game, heckled Jack about his weight. He also made a racist slur about Jack carrying a watermelon.

When Jack later took the field, he spotted the pitcher standing on the steps to his team's dugout. Jack had a clear shot, and he fired a baseball directly at Burdette's head.

He missed, and the ball bounced off the back wall of the dugout.

"I threw it at him because I wanted to hit him right between the eyes," Jack later explained. "He was calling me names, and I won't stand for that."

He was right about that. Since 1949, he had fought against unfair treatment on the diamond. He had battled extra hard when he detected racism in the words and actions of players, coaches, managers, and umpires. Perhaps there's a case to be made that his fighting intensified after Branch Rickey left the Dodgers organization in 1950. Most times while fighting back, Jack kept his temper in check, but sometimes he simply exploded.

"Jackie" had returned to being "Jack."

SEVENTEEN

WINNING THE
WORLD SERIES

J ack pressed his well-worn cleats into the soft padding of third base.
It was a comfortable feeling, but a desperate moment.

It was the top of the eighth inning in game one of the 1955 World
Series. The Yankees were ahead by two runs, and the Dodgers had two
outs.

Brooklyn had made it to the series five times, in 1941, 1947, 1949,
1952, and 1953, each time squaring off against the Yankees, each time
going down to defeat.

Would this year be the same old story? Would "dem Bums," as fans
fondly called them, have to "wait till next year," as their motto put it?

Yankee Stadium was tightly packed with 63,869 anxious fans.

Eyeing the pitcher, Jack flapped his arms out and took a slight
lead.

By now, his base-stealing skills were the stuff of legend, but he was
no longer in his prime years. Attempting a steal was riskier than ever.

Plus, stealing home was not the safest way to score a run, especially
with two outs. Few in the stadium, including Yankee pitcher Whitey
Ford, believed that Jack would try such a brazen play.

Extending his lead, Jack saw that Ford wasn't giving him much of a look.

Jack broke into an all-out sprint.

Ford gunned the ball to catcher Yogi Berra.

Jack slid hard.

Umpire Bill Summers hovered over the slide.

"It's close," a broadcaster announced.

When the dust settled, Summers spread his arms wide.

"Safe!"

The stadium shook with cheers and jeers.

The Yankees dugout exploded with rage.

Berra ripped off his catcher's mask, got into the umpire's face, shouted, and kicked the dirt.

Grinning, Jack trotted back to the dugout.

It was a history-making play. Before that moment, there had been only eight thefts of home in the World Series, and since that moment, no MLB player has ever stolen home in the championship games. "A successful steal of home is the rarest offense gesture in World Series competition," a sportswriter noted.

As for Jack, he acknowledged that "a steal of home like that in the eighth is usually not a good play."

He also refused to give Berra a fraction of an inch.

"I was safe—no doubt in my mind at all," he said.

Now back in their seats, Brooklyn fans let out a collective sigh of relief. The team still had life. More important, Jack noted, "whether it was because of my stealing home or not, the team had a new fire."

It would not be enough to overcome the Yankees that afternoon, but over the course of the next six games, the fire continued to build, though it took a while for the flames to soar high.

Game two proved to be a dismal replay of game one, dampening

Challenging Yankee catcher Yogi Berra in Game One of the 1955 World Series

Moments later, Yogi Berra tears into umpire Bill Summers after Jack was called safe at home.

the spirits of Brooklyn fans even further. But in game three, the Dodgers roared back, winning 8–3. Jack's two-hit performance included a double that landed him back on third base, where he distracted the pitcher by threatening another steal of home.

Sportswriter Jimmy Cannon asked Jack what had propelled the team to victory. Without hesitation, he credited a short speech given by manager Walter Alston in a pregame meeting.

"All Walter said," Jack recalled, "was we're the better ball club. All he told us was to play. It was all that stuff about the Yankees. It was short and right to the point."

Jack's appreciation for Alston's words might have surprised those who knew the history between the two men.

Earlier that spring, during the pre-season, Jack had wanted to play regularly at third base, but Alston refused him. Angry, Jack publicly criticized his manager, an act that would have been unthinkable for "Jackie" in 1947.

Sportswriter Gayle Talbot accused Jack of "insubordination such as seldom reaches the public print." Talbot added that the open rebellion would have far-reaching consequences: "No matter what apologies are made by Robinson—and he has said that he simply doesn't know how to talk to Alston—nothing is going to make them like or respect each other again, and the Dodgers' chances will suffer accordingly."

Talbot was wrong. Despite the rocky start, Jack and Alston found a way to work together so well that the Dodgers captured the division pennant and won game three of the World Series.

Building on their momentum, the Dodgers won the next two games at home, taking a commanding 3–2 lead into game six at Yankee Stadium. But "dem Bums" faltered as the Yanks cruised to a 5–1 lead.

Just after the game, sportswriter Jimmy Cannon saw that Jack was "irritated." But he also observed that Jack was "a man goaded by violent ambition," and that "desire" counted as much as skill in baseball. Because of that, Cannon said, it would be foolish to count the Dodgers out.

Jack did not play in game seven. To this day, the reason for his benching is unclear. Was it his bad knees? A sore ankle? A strained Achilles? Something not physical? MLB writer Barry M. Bloom says: "The real reason why Robinson didn't play . . . probably went with Robinson and Alston to their graves."

Still, even without Jack, the Dodgers rose to the occasion, scoring two runs from the fiery bats of Roy Campanella, Pee Wee Reese, and Gil Hodges. But the brilliant star of the day was southpaw Johnny Podres. The young pitcher tossed a breathtaking no-hitter, leaving the Yanks stunned—and defeated.

The Dodgers erupted, descending on Podres and cheering at the tops of their lungs.

Brooklyn fans were just as ecstatic. They poured into the streets. They threw their caps into the air. They gave one another bear hugs. They drank too much beer.

Sportswriters lauded Podres's ace pitching, but they also heaped praise on Jack when commenting on the overall series.

"His hair is gray," observed the *Boston Globe*. "His body is almost portly. And he can't run the way he did in his days in the Negro league." But "he showed his teammates, he showed his opponents, he showed a nation—that the Dodgers can beat the Yankees."

Jack's World Series performance, especially his electrifying steal of home, would have capped a brilliant end to his extraordinary career.

But shortly after the sweet victory, he told the media that he hoped to return to the Dodgers for another year.

"With the world championship and all, they may not feel so badly toward the old boy," he said.

The aging veteran did indeed return, and "dem Bums" lost to the Yankees in the 1956 World Series. Now, with his body starting to break down, Jack wasn't so sure he wanted to say "Wait till next year."

PART IV

CIVIL RIGHTS

EIGHTEEN

MARCHING FOR INTEGRATED SCHOOLS

Jack receiving the Spingarn Medal from TV variety show host Ed Sullivan, right, and NAACP leader Roy Wilkins

On December 8, 1956, five hundred invited guests poured into the swanky Roosevelt Hotel in Midtown Manhattan. They were there to honor Jack Roosevelt Robinson as he received the NAACP's Spingarn Medal, an annual award for "the highest or noblest achievement of an American Negro."

The luncheon was a lavish affair, and everyone was dressed in their finest. Jack was in his best suit, and Rachel wore a stunning string of pearls. Major personalities from entertainment, business, politics, and sports dined at beautifully set tables with starched white tablecloths.

Famous television host Ed Sullivan bestowed the medal on his good friend and golf partner. Now sporting a bit of white hair, Jack smiled as Sullivan placed the ribbon over his head.

The written citation that accompanied the medal praised Jack's historic role in Major League Baseball, but it also lauded his "civic consciousness," his actions as a "citizen of democracy."

Jack no doubt appreciated the citation because it reflected the way he thought of himself—as much more than the star baseball player who cracked MLB's color barrier.

"Today marks the high point of my career," he said upon receiving the award. "To be honored in this way by the NAACP means more than anything that has happened to me before. That is because the NAACP, to me, represents everything a man should stand for: for human dignity, for brotherhood, for fair play."

Five days later, Jack's life took a dramatic turn. Walter O'Malley, the owner of the Brooklyn Dodgers, traded him to the New York Giants.

The baseball world was stunned.

Jack and Branch Rickey, second from left, at an NAACP event in 1957

The Giants were the crosstown rivals of the Dodgers, and the trade seemed disrespectful of Jack's wholehearted devotion to the Dodgers.

Jack was surprised but not shocked. He and O'Malley had never gotten along.

Rather than agreeing to the trade, which he saw as a vicious insult, Jack simply retired from the game he had transformed.

It was not a happy ending.

WHY DID JACK RETIRE FROM BASEBALL?

Historians have suggested that Jack had several reasons for deciding to retire. What do you think? Did Jack retire because

- his body was wearing down?
- his statistics had started to fall?
- he wasn't receiving as much playing time as he wanted?
- he didn't want to play for the Giants?
- he was tired of ongoing racism in MLB?
- he detested playing for Dodger owner Walter O'Malley?
- he wanted to make more money?
- he already had the Chock Full o'Nuts job lined up?

Were other reasons at play? In 1962, Jack wrote: "I left baseball because my integrity was challenged by one executive in the game." He never publicly explained what he meant by that statement. What do you think he meant?

But Jack was already poised to make history once again. Shortly after his retirement, he announced that he had accepted a job as vice president and director of personnel at Chock Full o'Nuts, a chain of

Mr. Jack R. Robinson, vice president at Chock Full o'Nuts, in 1957

coffee shops owned by white business leader William Black. This marked the first time in US history that a Black person became vice president of a major US corporation.

The job provided Jack with a handsome salary and a company car. Even better, Black gave Jack the freedom to use company time to volunteer for the NAACP. This was important because Jack had also accepted an offer to chair the NAACP's Freedom Fund Drive, a national campaign to increase membership and raise $1,000,000.

When accepting the position, Jack insisted on doing more than lending his name and photo for campaign letters, flyers, and posters. "If my name was going to be involved, then I wanted to be involved as much as possible," he said.

Jack resolved to fight for civil rights at least as hard as he'd fought to win the World Series. His new battle for freedom had begun, and it would last for the rest of his life.

Jack took a nationwide tour for the Freedom Fund in 1957. He loved speaking to the crowds, and they loved listening to their hero. At first, his speeches were brief, about five or ten minutes long, but by the end of the tour, he was giving captivating talks that lasted half an hour.

He often spoke about his recent shift into civil rights work. "There was a time when I erred in being complacent," he said. "Then I realized my responsibilities to my race and to my country."

At a rally in Los Angeles, Jack sold kisses. To no one's surprise, a long line quickly formed.

On October 25, 1958, Jack donned a jacket and tie in his hotel room in Washington, DC. He was getting ready to lead a student march demanding an immediate end to racial segregation in public schools.

Eleven-year-old Jackie Jr. also wore a jacket and tie, and he proudly joined his father at the head of the march down Constitution Avenue, a wide street that runs from the US Capitol to the Lincoln Memorial. Two other famous people—Coretta Scott King and the singer Harry Belafonte—also led the way.

About 7,500 young people fell into line behind the leaders, chanting, "Why wait? Integrate!" Another favorite chant was "Two, four, six, eight! We want to integrate!" The funniest one was "Phooey on Faubus." That was about Orval Faubus, the Arkansas governor who opposed racial integration in public schools.

About halfway through the march, a smaller group peeled off and marched to the White House, where they hoped to deliver a petition to president Dwight Eisenhower. When a guard rebuffed them, they silently picketed the White House for half an hour. By this point, the rest of the marchers, now numbering ten thousand, had made their way to the Lincoln Memorial for a protest rally.

Jack loved the sight of all the young protesters, and although he beamed as he headed to the microphone to deliver his speech, he had something serious on his mind: the angry white people in Little Rock, Arkansas, who had recently used violence to prevent Black kids from entering all-white schools.

"You have demonstrated to the world that Little Rock is not America!" Jack proudly told the student marchers. "I'm sorry that the President hasn't demonstrated by his actions that he agrees with this demonstration."

The students roared their support and voted to hold another

Students getting ready for the Youth March for Integrated Schools, Washington, DC, 1958

march the following spring to mark the fifth anniversary of *Brown v. Board of Education*, the historic Supreme Court ruling that racial segregation in public schools was unconstitutional.

As the Youth March for Integrated Schools ended, numerous students swarmed around Jack and asked for his autograph. Jack might have retired from MLB, but he was still their hero in their own fight for first-class citizenship.

Jack helped to lead a second march, too. This one had twenty-six thousand students, and the presence of Martin Luther King Jr. made the day extra special. For Jack, though, the highlight was when the student protesters cheered thunderously as he accepted an award for his contributions to the cause of racial integration.

Jack's stature as a civil rights leader was now growing by leaps and bounds, and six days after the march, *New York Post* editor James Wechsler announced that he had just signed Jack to write a triweekly column that would be distributed to newspapers across the country.

This, too, was a historic first. It marked the first time that a major newspaper owned and operated by white people had signed a Black person to write a nationally syndicated column.

As an outspoken man, Jack was thrilled at the chance to share his opinions on any topic of his choosing—especially civil rights.

Jack inspecting the ashes of Mount Olive Baptist Church in Sasser, Georgia, one of three African-American churches in the state destroyed by arson in August and September 1962 after being used as voter registration meeting sites

NINETEEN

EXTINGUISHING HATRED

J ack anxiously waited for news about the 1962 election results for the National Baseball Hall of Fame. It was his first year of eligibility, and his election was far from certain.

Sports fans suggested that the temper he had shown on the baseball diamond would prevent members of the Baseball Writers' Association of America from voting for him. Jack had something to say about that.

"I directed my 'fiery' temper against violations of my personal dignity and civil rights and the civil rights of the people for whom I have such deep concern," he wrote in his newspaper column. "If I honestly qualify and if I am refused the honor because I fought and argued for the principles in which I deeply believe, so be it."

He had nothing to worry about. On January 23, 1962, Jack was elected to the Hall of Fame along with ace pitcher Bob Feller, also eligible for the first time. Their elections made history—no other players in their first year of eligibility had ever been selected.

Surprised and thrilled, Jack used his election to share a message of hope with young people feeling down on themselves.

"I just want to say that if this can happen to a guy whose parents

Branch Rickey, Jack, Rachel Robinson, and Mallie Robinson at the National Baseball Hall of Fame in Cooperstown, New York

were virtually slaves, a guy from a broken home, a guy whose mother worked as a domestic from sun-up to sun-down for a number of years; if this can happen to someone who, in his early years, was a delinquent and who learned that he had to change his life — then it can happen to you kids out there who think that life is against you."

On July 20, 1962, more than six hundred people packed the Starlight Roof, an ornate room in the Waldorf Astoria Hotel in New York City, to honor Jack upon his induction into the Hall of Fame.

His good friend New York governor Nelson Rockefeller offered a special tribute, saying that while Jack had a batting average of .311, he also had "a lifetime batting average of 1,000 as a fine human being.

"He became a living fulfillment of the American dream, a hero of the struggle to make American democracy a genuine reality for every American."

Jack was deeply touched by the event, and tears welled in his eyes as he rose to thank everyone in attendance. "The only hope I ever have is that I never let you down," he told them.

After the dinner, Martin Luther King Jr. published a tribute in his popular newspaper column. Jack, he said, had earned the right to speak his mind as he saw fit.

"He has the right—more rightly—because back in the days when integration wasn't fashionable, he underwent the trauma and the humiliation and the loneliness which comes with being a pilgrim walking the lonesome byways toward the high road of Freedom. He was a sit-inner before the sit-ins, a freedom rider before the Freedom Rides."

One month later, Jack jumped on a plane and headed to Albany, Georgia, where Dr. King was leading a protest to abolish racial segregation. The civil rights leader had asked him to visit the small city and help build the morale of weary and worn activists.

It was a hot and humid day, but more than a thousand Black people turned out to see their hero. Jack was visibly moved as he listened to elementary-age children singing "We Shall Overcome," the theme song of the civil rights movement, in his honor.

After delivering a passionate speech, he traveled to nearby Sasser, Georgia, to survey the still-hot ashes of Mount Olive Baptist Church, one of three Black churches burned to the ground for registering Black voters. Angry white people in the area feared that the right to vote would result in Black people winning political power.

Still wearing his suit, Jack stood atop the smoldering ashes. He felt as if he was attending "the funeral of a church," he said.

Next to him, Mount Olive's members, with tears running down their faces, comforted one another. An elderly Black woman in a homespun dress lovingly patted the back of a devastated friend.

"It really makes you want to cry deep down in your heart," Jack told a reporter.

The scene of devastation moved him so much that he resolved to help raise funds to rebuild the churches. He also pledged $100 on the spot.

Shortly after he returned to New York, Jack received a call from Dr. King, thanking him for his trip to the Albany Movement and asking him to chair the fundraising campaign for the churches. Together, the two friends set up the Church Fund, and before long, Jack had collected a little more than $20,000 of the $50,000 that he eventually raised.

Dr. King praised Jack's wholehearted commitment.

"There is little doubt that before many days, out of the ashes and ruins of those churches ... there will rise brick and mortar and steel because there is a man named Jack Roosevelt Robinson," King wrote.

He was right. Two years later, three brand-new churches stood proudly atop the ashes and ruins.

TWENTY

BACKING THE BIRMINGHAM STUDENTS

Birmingham students seeking protection from supercharged fire hoses, May 1963

Jack's blood boiled as he read the news from Birmingham. Thousands of Black students, some of them still in elementary school, were now under arrest for taking part in peaceful marches for civil rights. Although Jack was irate, he also felt proud of the kids for demanding an end to racial segregation in their city.

He well knew that Birmingham, like most places in the South, was an unfriendly and dangerous place for Black people. Public schools, sports fields, movie theaters, swimming pools, and even cemeteries were racially segregated. Worse, white police officers often harassed

A snarling police dog attacking a seventeen-year-old protester in Birmingham on May 4, 1963

Black people for no real reason, and members of the Ku Klux Klan dynamited Black homes and churches.

What Jack hadn't known, until he read the news, was that Birmingham's Black students had had enough. They had grown sick and tired of all the abuse, and they had shouted "Yes!" at the tops of their lungs when Martin Luther King Jr. invited them to join his protests for freedom.

On the morning of May 2, 1963, about a thousand Black students poured into Sixteenth Street Baptist Church to prepare for a day of protest. Chatting nervously, they pushed one another as they slid onto the hard wooden pews in the sanctuary. Before long, they started to belt out their new favorite freedom song:

> *Ain't gonna let segregation turn me 'round,*
> *Turn me 'round, turn me 'round.*
> *Ain't gonna let segregation turn me 'round.*
> *I'm gonna keep on a-walkin', keep on a-talkin'.*
> *Marchin' on to freedom land.*

The adults in the room—Dr. King's advisers—beamed at the sight of so many kids. It felt so good to hear their joyful sounds, to see their fresh faces, and to feel their energetic spirit. The Birmingham protest movement felt alive once again.

Around noon, the adults organized the students into groups of fifty and sent them out the massive red door, one group at a time, with instructions to march to the city hall. Some of the students held home-made protest signs, some walked hand in hand, and some skipped and clapped.

It didn't take long before they spotted Birmingham's police force. The officers were in a foul mood as the peaceful protesters walked toward them, and they angrily barked that everyone was under arrest.

Before the day was over, about nine hundred had been arrested and jailed for protesting for freedom. Being in jail was frightening, but the students found great comfort in singing and praying together.

On the second day of the Children's Crusade, as it came to be called, thousands of other students gathered at Kelly Ingram Park, waving their picket signs, singing freedom songs, and clapping and dancing. Birmingham safety commissioner Eugene "Bull" Connor—who was well-known for brutalizing Black people—also showed up, with police officers and firefighters in tow.

Connor ordered his firefighters to turn their hoses on the kids. As the men opened the nozzles, chaos broke out. The supercharged hoses blasted the students off their feet, leaving them with bruised bones and organs. One girl suffered permanent hearing loss.

Connor also instructed his police officers to sic their snarling German shepherds on the kids. A dog named "Nigger" was especially mean. Boys and girls screamed in pain as the vicious dogs tore into their flesh. One dog lunged at a child's throat, and others bit arms and legs and stomachs and backs. By the end of the day, more than 1,900 students had been arrested, with many of them jailed in pigpens at the city's fairgrounds.

At home in Connecticut, Jack was furious. The photos of police officers and firefighters assaulting Black kids sickened him, and he immediately sent a telegram to President John F. Kennedy. "The revolution that is taking place in this country cannot be squelched by police dogs or high-power hoses," he wrote, adding that the president should seize control in Birmingham and protect its Black citizens.

Around this same time, Dr. King reached out to Jack and asked him to visit Birmingham. The students had sacrificed so much, and King thought that his good friend would help give them the strength and courage required to continue their fight for freedom.

Jack accepted the invitation without hesitation, and he soon told news reporters about the trip. "I don't like to be bitten by dogs, because I'm a coward," he said. "I don't like to go to jail, either, because, as I say, I'm a coward. But we've got to show Martin Luther King that we are behind him."

The flight to Birmingham was uneventful, but upon departing the plane, Jack learned of a death threat against him. Although long accustomed to such warnings, he still found them unnerving. Still, he would never let a death threat turn him around.

Walking down the airport's main corridor, Jack waved to a group of twenty-five Black janitors holding brooms. Unknown to him, the job of this broom brigade was to sweep away anyone who dared to threaten their honored guest.

Just outside the airport exit was a police cruiser waiting to escort the car designated for Jack and his hosts. Jack was no doubt surprised to see the officers, but he also understood that Bull Connor wanted this so-called "outside agitator" out of the city as fast as possible.

The police cruiser stopped first at Fifth Street Baptist Church, one of the city's largest Black churches, where a lively crowd of two thousand Black people, including Dr. King, was in the middle of singing "Freedom," an emotionally powerful song written especially for the Birmingham Movement.

Pandemonium broke out as soon as Jack stepped inside the sanctuary.

"Jackie!" the crowd shouted, surging forward to get close to him.

Standing behind the pulpit, Jack quieted everyone and thanked them for waking up the conscience of America. To the crowd's delight, he also ripped into Bull Connor for bullying and brutalizing innocent kids.

"You can love them if you want to, but me, I simply can't do it," he said about Bull Connor and his troops. A news reporter noted that Dr. King—who always called for love and nonviolence—had a pained look on his face when Jack said that.

The second rally was held at Pilgrim Baptist Church, where two thousand kids screamed and cheered even louder than the adults had. They craned their necks to catch a glimpse of their hero, and some rushed to touch his hand, while others whistled as if they were at the World Series.

After several minutes of sheer chaos, Jack told the students that he was there to honor them and their

Jack talking with Dr. King during his visit to Birmingham on May 14, 1963

sacrifice. "I don't think you realize down here in Birmingham what you mean to us up there in New York," he said. (Although Jack lived in Connecticut, he worked in Manhattan, and many of his friends in the civil rights movement lived and worked in New York City.)

Jack loved interacting with kids, and rather than just speaking at them, he also posed a couple of questions. Two thousand hands shot high in the air when he asked how many of the students had gone to jail. Jack shook his head in amazement.

"All those of you who saw pictures of the dogs tearing the flesh of Negroes, raise your hands," he added.

This time, no one responded, and Jack looked puzzled. Then a nine-year-old student bravely stood up and said, "Mr. Robinson, we didn't see the pictures of the dogs—but we saw the dogs!"

Everyone laughed, including Jack, who later learned that the city's white newspapers had refused to print photographs showing white police officers terrorizing Black kids. The photos had traveled across the world, as far as Russia and China, but Birmingham's white editors had censored them.

Jack praised the students once again, and he shook a lot of hands before leaving for his overnight accommodations at the nearby A. G. Gaston Motel. He certainly wasn't looking forward to going to the motel, because just a week earlier, when Dr. King had stayed there, local racists had bombed part of it.

Jack's hosts noticed a concerned look on his face at the motel. "Don't worry about any bombs here," they said. "Lightning never strikes the same place twice."

But four months later, lightning would strike Birmingham's kids again, and Jack would be back, angrier than ever.

TWENTY-ONE

MARCHING ON WASHINGTON

Jack and Rachel hosting an "Afternoon of Jazz" at their home in Stamford, Connecticut, in 1963

Back home in Stamford, Connecticut, Jack told Rachel that Dr. King needed money to bail student protesters out of jail. The couple soon decided to hold an "Afternoon of Jazz," a fundraising concert on their expansive lawn.

With help from friends and family, Jack and Rachel called musicians, pitched a big tent, built a stage, sent invitations, created a menu, and made sure there were enough bathrooms.

The response was overwhelming. About five hundred people showed up to listen to the jazz greats who volunteered their talents.

Dizzy Gillespie's cheeks inflated as he blew his trumpet, and Duke Ellington smiled broadly as he pounded the piano keys and led his world-famous band.

Jack wore an apron and sold food to the crowd, while Rachel peddled raffle tickets for cakes baked by her mother.

At the end of the day, Jack and Rachel were worn out but happy. The "jam session" had raised more than $15,000.

Three days later, Jack was no longer smiling. He had just learned that Harlem residents had booed Dr. King and pelted him with eggs as he arrived at Salem Methodist Church to deliver an evening speech.

Dr. King was shaken and disappointed. Speaking before an audience of two thousand, he said, "I can't understand what my colored brothers have against me."

Local police officers faulted Minister Malcolm X, an important leader in the Nation of Islam, for inspiring the egg throwing. The Associated Negro Press also reported that on the night prior to Dr. King's visit, Malcolm had urged his followers to "go up there to Salem Church tomorrow and let Uncle Tom [King] know that we are against him and do not believe what he preaches."

Malcolm X opposed Dr. King's teachings about nonviolence and racial integration. Unlike King, he believed that Black people had a right to defend themselves with physical force and that white people were evil and would never allow Black people to be fully integrated into society. Black people would be far better off in a separate state where they could build their own businesses and governments, he said.

Malcolm was a charismatic leader, and he was popular among

Black youths in cities like New York, Chicago, and Washington, DC. They believed that leaders like Dr. King, Roy Wilkins of the NAACP, and Jack were too submissive—too patient with injustice and not tough enough when dealing with racists.

THE NATION OF ISLAM

The Nation of Islam is a religious movement and organization founded by Wallace D. Fard Muhammad in 1930. Its teachings and practices blend traditional Islam with Black nationalism. Members of the Nation worship God as Allah, and they study and practice lessons taught by the Prophet Muhammad, as revealed in the Koran. Members also embrace Black pride and advocate for Black separatism and self-sufficiency in politics and economics. Elijah Muhammad, Farrad Muhammad's disciple, assumed leadership of the Nation in 1934, and in the late 1950s and early 1960s, Minister Malcolm X was its most popular spokesperson.

Malcolm X speaking to a crowd of supporters in Harlem in 1963

Jack did not appreciate Malcolm X or his teachings.

Although Malcolm denied that Black Muslims were responsible for the egg throwing, Jack blamed him "for helping to create a climate in the Harlem community which made it possible for such a despicable incident to occur . . .

"Malcolm has just as much right to be opposed to Dr. King as anyone else," he said. "I do not think it is fair, however, for Malcolm to continue to make the kind of statements which incite people to attempt to dishonor a man of the integrity of Dr. King."

Jack added that if Malcolm was so troubled by Dr. King's philosophy, and by the US government, he should practice what he preached.

"Malcolm X and his organization believe in separation. They have every right to. If they want to go off into some all-black community, why don't they just go?"

Those were fighting words, and the battle between the two men would erupt again before the end of the year. Before that would happen, though, one of the best days of Jack's life was right around the corner.

Thirteen-year-old Sharon Robinson was anxious about the upcoming March on Washington for Jobs and Freedom. She had watched television reports of the Birmingham officials turning dogs and hoses on Black students, and she was concerned for her safety. Her older brother, Jackie Jr., and younger brother, David, also wondered about the possibility of violence, and the three siblings drilled their father with questions.

"Will the police use fire hoses to stop us?" they asked.

"Are we going to jail?"

"This is not Birmingham," Jack replied. "There will be no fire hoses or dogs, and hopefully no arrests. This is supposed to be a peaceful march, and I expect everyone, including the police, will be on their best behavior."

What Jack may not have expected was for the march to culminate in one of the defining moments in American history—Martin Luther King's "I Have a Dream" speech.

The Robinsons arrived at the Willard Hotel in downtown Washington, DC, on August 26, 1963, a hot and humid day that was typical for the city at this time of year. They were extra excited when they learned that Dr. King was staying at the same hotel.

On the following day, while Rachel took the kids on a tour of the White House, march organizer Bayard Rustin invited Jack to speak to the crowd before the official start of the march.

Jack was thrilled.

On the morning of August 28, a young man from Howard University arrived at the hotel to escort the Robinsons to an area designated for special guests. After a short while, Jack walked to a stage near the Washington Monument to greet the swelling crowd.

When he approached the microphone, the crowd erupted in cheers. Smiling and waving, Jack welcomed everyone and said that he and the Robinson family would march alongside them.

"I know all of us are going to go away feeling ... we cannot turn back," he added.

The march from the Washington Monument to the Lincoln Memorial began at around noon. Jack walked with his big arm around David. Marching next to Rachel, Sharon felt as if she was part of a wave, something much bigger than herself.

Many of the marchers held signs that read, WE MARCH FOR

Jack with son David at the March on Washington for Jobs and Freedom,
August 28, 1963

INTEGRATED SCHOOLS *NOW!*; WE MARCH FOR JOBS FOR ALL *NOW!*; WE
DEMAND DECENT HOUSING *NOW!*; and WE DEMAND AN END TO BIAS *NOW!*

It was another hot day, and the heat caused Sharon to faint. Rachel
took her to a first-aid tent, where she recovered by drinking forti-
fied water and eating peanut butter crackers. She and Rachel made

it to the Lincoln Memorial just in time for the start of the program at 2:00 P.M.

Camilla Williams, a Black opera star, sang the national anthem, and Dr. King gave the closing speech. At first, Dr. King's speech seemed like nothing special; even his voice sounded flat. But then he began to share his powerful dream for the country.

"I have a dream," he said. "I have a dream that . . . one day right there in Alabama, little black boys and black girls will be able to join hands with little white boys and white girls as sisters and brothers. I have a dream today!"

After Dr. King finished speaking, the crowd of 250,000 roared. Many cried. Others laughed with sheer joy. It was a defining moment in world history.

"I have never been so proud to be a Negro," Jack said after the march. "I have never been so proud to be an American."

The sight of Black people and white people coming together to demand jobs and freedom had filled him with immense pride.

"One had to be deeply moved as he stood, watching Negroes and whites, marching hand in hand, singing songs for freedom," he said. "What a beautiful picture we gave to the world."

At the same time, Jack sounded an alarm about politicians who had made disparaging remarks about the march and who now announced they would block President Kennedy's call for a new civil rights law.

If the racists succeeded, Jack warned, "I am not so certain that nonviolence will win the day."

The horrific bombing of Sixteenth Street Baptist Church killed four girls on September 15, 1963 (Birmingham Public Library Archives)

TWENTY-TWO

WARRING WITH MALCOLM X

Members of Sixteenth Street Baptist Church screamed in horror when they discovered the bodies of four Black girls killed in the blast on that September Sunday—Addie Mae Collins, Denise McNair, Carole Robertson, and Cynthia Wesley.

The deafening explosion left twenty-one other worshippers bloodied and dazed. Precious stained-glass windows were shattered, and nearby cars were crushed. It was the twenty-first bombing in eight years in Birmingham, or "Bombingham," as some called it.

As word about the explosion spread, Black people from across the city showed up. Some were determined to exact revenge on the white terrorists who had dynamited the church. Reverend John Cross, the church's minister, sobbed as he pleaded for everyone to return to their homes peacefully.

Jack had a different reaction. He was angry, and in his newspaper column, he used a popular civil rights song, "If I Had a Hammer," to express his rage.

"If I had been a parent in Birmingham on a Sunday morning which was shattered by a detonation more vicious than any ever released by Hitler in Nazi Germany—and if, in the ruins of that bombing, one of my children had been found, I know what I would have done with that hammer," he wrote.

Jack was not a pacifist.

"God bless Dr. Martin Luther King," he added. "But I'm afraid he would have lost me as a potential disciple of his credo of non-violence."

Right after the explosion, financial donations began to pour into the church, and Black leaders established a fundraising committee. As a veteran fundraiser, Jack was asked to serve as co-chair. It was an opportunity for him to constructively channel his fury.

"Yes, I'll be happy to serve," he said. "The bombing made me physically sick."

Something else sickened Jack near the end of 1963 — Malcolm X's growing popularity among Black people. Once again, the two engaged in a fierce battle of words.

In his newspaper column, Jack chided Malcolm for refusing to lead the civil rights movement in the South. Malcolm was too cowardly to leave Harlem, he suggested.

Malcolm fired back, accusing Jack of being subservient to "the White Man" and of being the "right" kind of Black man, one quick to criticize Black militants who demanded freedom without delay.

The war of words continued.

"Coming from you, an attack is a tribute," Jack replied. "Personally, I reject your racist views. I reject your dream of a separate state," he added.

"Negroes are not fooled by your vicious theories that they are dying for freedom to please the white man. Negroes are fighting for freedom and rejecting your racism because we feel our stake in America is worth fighting for."

In conclusion, Jack said he was glad that Malcolm had few followers. "I hate to think of where we would be if we followed your leadership. Strictly in my personal opinion, it is a sick leadership which should rightfully be rejected by the vast majority of Americans."

Angry Malcolm X blasts Robinson

WASHINGTON

In a recent newspaper column, Jackie Robinson was critical of the Black Muslim movement. In response, Malcolm X, No. 2 leader in the movement, accused Robinson of attempting to mislead the minority group politically.

He also defended a recent attack on Ralph Bunche, declaring that he criticized Bunche in self - defense after the UN Under Secretary General opened fire on the Black Muslims.

Part of Malcolm X's reply follows:

* * *

"DEAR good friend, Jackie Roosevelt Robinson: You became a great baseball player after your white boss (Mr. Rickey) lifted you to the Major Leagues. You proved that your white boss had chosen the 'right' colored person by getting plenty of hits, stealing plenty of bases, winning many games and bringing much money through the gates and into the pockets of your white boss.

even in those days against your own kind. You let them sic you on Paul Robeson.

"You let your white boss send you before a congressional hearing in Washington, D.C. (the capitol of Segregationville) to dispute and condemn Paul Robeson, because he has these guilty American whites frightened silly.

"Your white boss sent you to Washington to assure all the worried white folks that colored people were still thankful to the Great White Father for bringing us to to America, that colored persons were grateful to America (despite our not being treated as full citizens), and that colored people would still lay down our lives to defend this white country (though this same government wasn't ready nor willing to defend colored people) even in those days, Jackie!

"In this same recent column you also accused me and Dr. Powell of misleading our people. Aren't you the same ex - baseball player who tried to "mislead" color-

Malcolm fought back when Jack criticized his views about racial segregation and violence. (Afro-American, December 7, 1963)

Malcolm left the Nation of Islam in March 1964. Thereafter known as Brother Malcolm, he called a press conference on March 12 and announced the formation of a new movement dedicated to advancing Black nationalism and reshaping the civil rights movement.

"White people will be shocked when they discover that the passive little Negro they had known turns out to be a roaring lion," he predicted.

Under his leadership, he said, Black nationalists would control the politics of their own communities, running for office and electing themselves. They would own, manage, and shop at their own businesses. And they would refuse the nonviolence embraced by Dr. King.

"It is criminal to teach a man not to defend himself when he is the constant victim of brutal attacks," Malcolm declared.

"In areas where our people are the constant victims of brutality and the Government seems unable or unwilling to protect them, we should form rifle clubs that can be used to defend our lives and our property in times of emergency."

Malcolm's words alarmed Jack. The thought of rifle clubs concerned him because he knew that armed white people far outnumbered Black people with guns. Taking up arms would be disastrous for Black folks.

Hoping to stem Malcolm's growing popularity, Jack called for civil rights leaders to come together and issue a collective statement that declared their opposition to Malcolm. But Jack's influence was limited. No one called a meeting, and there was no collective statement.

On April 13, 1964, Malcolm began a pilgrimage to Mecca, the holy city of Islam, that turned out to be personally transformative. His vision of Islam deepened and widened when he saw different races and ethnicities worshiping together peacefully and respectfully.

Back home, Malcolm no longer called for Black people to segregate themselves from all white people. He now envisioned building a racially inclusive movement that would seek to eliminate white supremacy.

Jack balked.

"We would really be cutting our own throats if large numbers of our people listened to and followed the confused and confusing leadership which Malcolm projects," Jack said.

"What does this man really think?" Jack also asked with a snarky tone. "What is he really after? Money? Power?"

On February 21, 1965, Malcolm X was shot and killed while speaking to about four hundred followers at the Audubon Ballroom in Manhattan. The assassins might have murdered him in retaliation for leaving the Nation of Islam and starting his own organization.

Jack and Rachel were vacationing in Miami when they received the news, and Jack decided he would write about Malcolm in his next newspaper column. He was careful not to pretend that the two had been friends.

"But I have always respected the man as one who said what he believed," Jack wrote. "The courage to do that is, in my mind, one of the most vital qualities a human being can possess."

Jack also predicted that Malcolm's assassination would add to his lasting influence.

"The crack of those bullets which took his life will have many echoes," he said. "The case of Malcolm X is not closed."

He was right. A year later, Stokely Carmichael and Black militants in the Student Nonviolent Coordinating Committee, a civil rights group for young people, ignited the Black Power movement. Influenced by Malcolm, the movement embraced Black separatism and the use of force in self-defense.

Jack often criticized the movement and said that Black people can best express Black power by using "our ballot and our dollars wisely"—by supporting pro–civil rights candidates and businesses.

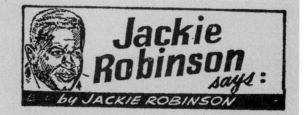

Martyr Malcolm

MIAMI—(ANPI)—A little blue went out of the sky and a bit of warmth left the sun here, where we were relaxing and playing golf—when the news came that a hail of bullets had silenced Malcolm X

When they murdered Malcolm, they murdered not only a man but the precious freedom to talk, to speak one's mind to disagree.

Many times I have been on record in this column and elsewhere as being opposed to Malcolm's philosophy. But I have always respected the man as one who said what he believed. The courage to do that is, in my mind, one of the most vital qualities a human being can possess.

I have met Malcolm in debate and exchanged spirited letter with him in which he stuck to his guns and I to mine. Many of the statements he made about the problems faced by Negro people were nothing but the naked truth. However, we are often far apart in our opinions of how these problems should be faced.

An Articulate Voice Stilled

The person or persons who murdered Malcolm have stilled his articulate voice. But, in making him a martyr, they have only deepened whatever influence he may have had. In addition, they have generated a senseless brutal to war which sees black hands raised against black brothers at a time when we most need unity among black people.

So, in death, Malcolm X—and the X quality amout him which intrigued, attracted, fascinated and repelled — has been exaggerated as it was in life. The crack of those bullets which took his life will have many echoes. The case of Malcolm X is not closed.

Jack appreciated Malcolm's belief that civil rights leaders were too patient when dealing with racist leaders. (*New Journal and Guide*, March 20, 1965)

At the same time, though, Jack began to speak approvingly of Malcolm's impatience with the slow progress toward Black freedom. In the end, Jack turned to Malcolm as a source and symbol of strength, wisdom, and determination.

TWENTY-THREE

CRASHING THE WHITE MAN'S PARTY

Jack led the way as almost forty thousand protesters marched through San Francisco on July 13, 1964. They had come to the city for the Republican National Convention, and their protest targeted presidential candidate Barry Goldwater.

Jack had a history of supporting the Republican Party. He was attracted to it because it had been the party of Abraham Lincoln and other politicians who had fought against slavery. Plus, the modern Democratic Party was controlled by Southern politicians who opposed the civil rights movement.

Backing Republican candidates was also part of Jack's history. He had campaigned full-time for Richard Nixon in the 1960 presidential election, and his favorite politician was Governor Nelson Rockefeller of New York, a supporter of Black civil rights.

Goldwater was no Rockefeller. As a US senator, he refused to support federal civil rights legislation. He said that each state, even those ruled by Jim Crow, should be free to decide whether to create new civil rights laws.

Jack called Goldwater "a bigot" and "an advocate of white supremacy," and he warned that the Republican Party was becoming "a white man's party."

Jack speaking in San Francisco about his opposition to the nomination of Republican presidential candidate Barry Goldwater

The San Francisco march

was the largest in the country since the 1963 March on Washington for Jobs and Freedom.

Marching behind Jack, bead-wearing hippies flashed peace signs at spectators. Hundreds of other marchers, young and old, held homemade signs reading, WILL THE GOP BETRAY LINCOLN?, GOLDWATER IS A RAT FINK, and many other slogans. Some marchers pretended to be KKK leaders and carried signs that read: THE GRAND IMPERIAL WIZARDS FOR GOLDWATER.

While he enjoyed the march, Jack felt a throbbing pain in his knee, probably from an old sports injury. He limped to the sidewalk for a break, but soon headed back to the front. Nothing would keep him from leading the fight against Goldwater.

The march ended at City Hall, where the jam-packed crowd listened to a dozen anti-Goldwater speeches. Jack drew a thunderous ovation when he declared that Goldwater was "a bigot who will prevent us from moving forward."

A short time later, Jack walked through the doors of the Cow Palace, the site of the Republican National Convention. He was not an official delegate, but rather the invited guest of Governor Rockefeller. Just before business meetings started, Jack promised that there would be a "bloodbath" if the party nominated Goldwater.

Although he did not have the right to vote on convention matters,

Jack marching against the nomination of Barry Goldwater on July 13, 1964

Jack sought to be a forceful presence among the anti-Goldwater delegates. With Jack's encouragement, Black delegates tried to nominate a candidate who favored federal civil rights legislation. But that effort failed miserably; Goldwater and his supporters simply had too much power.

The delegates also lobbied for a strong civil rights section in the party's platform—its statement of principles, policies, and plans. But that didn't work, either.

The Black caucus, including Jack, then met behind closed doors and strategized about other protest options. One option was to walk out at the time of Goldwater's nomination—to walk off the convention floor, where all state delegations debated convention business, and out the doors.

Another idea was to stage a dramatic protest on the convention floor. While the group backed this idea, the plan collapsed when organizers failed to distribute protest signs in time for the nomination.

Making matters worse, Black delegates felt abused on the convention floor. George Fleming, one of the group's main leaders, shed tears when he told a reporter that Goldwater supporters had shoved, spat on, and cursed his colleagues using racist language.

Jack was disappointed, but there was one part of the convention proceedings that he loved—Governor Rockefeller's late-night speech.

The governor had lost to Goldwater in the race for the nomination, and he used his speech to share his vision for a racially inclusive party. Goldwater supporters booed and hissed as the governor spoke.

To emphasize his disgust with Goldwater, Jack stood with the Alabama delegation, one of the most pro-Goldwater groups, and loudly cheered for Governor Rockefeller.

"C'mon, Rocky!" he shouted.

A white delegate shot Jack a nasty look, jumped out of his seat, and lunged toward him. But his wife grabbed the man's arm and pulled him back before Jack could slug him.

"Turn him loose, lady, turn him loose!" Jack shouted.

"I was ready for him," he called. "I wanted him badly, but luckily for him he obeyed his wife."

Goldwater easily captured the nomination, and Jack campaigned for the Democratic candidate, Lyndon Johnson, who had become president after John F. Kennedy was assassinated. Johnson handily defeated Goldwater in the 1964 election and later signed new civil rights laws desegregating public facilities and ensuring Black people had the right to vote.

Pleased with the election, Jack shifted his attention to a new project— opening Freedom National Bank (FNB) in Harlem and becoming its chairman. Describing FNB, Jack said, "It is the only bank in Harlem which is interracially owned and operated. It is also the only bank in Harlem which is controlled mainly by Negroes."

Jack's leadership of the bank reflected his belief that Black Americans would never achieve first-class citizenship until they entered the mainstream of economic society and enjoyed the material benefits that white people had. FNB would help Black people do this because it offered affordable loans and reasonable mortgage rates—financial tools that white banks had denied them because of their skin color.

With Jack's help, the bank succeeded, making his own bank account grow. A capitalist at heart, he welcomed the opportunity to make money while helping people.

PART V

PATRIOTISM
AND FAMILY

TWENTY-FOUR

DEFENDING PEACE AND WAR

G o back to Africa, niggers!" the intruder shouted as he entered the banquet room.

The NAACP youth members put down their silverware, shocked by the commotion. They had been expecting a quiet dinner, followed by an awards ceremony hosted by their special guest, Jack Robinson. But the self-styled Nazi interloper put a glitch in all that.

Waving a swastika, the white man darted through the room and jumped onto the stage, grabbed the microphone, and again ranted about "sending all the niggers back to Africa."

Jack grew hot under the collar. "Not only was my anger rising," he recalled, "but I found that I was rising with every intention of letting this unexpected visitor have a good swift jab in the head."

The NAACP youth got to him before Jack did. "They didn't hit him," Jack explained. "They didn't maul him. They surrounded him, they took hold of him and hustled him out of the room." It was a classic nonviolent tactic.

"I will be very honest with you," Jack later explained. "I am not nonviolent in such circumstances."

But he was deeply proud of the NAACP youths.

One year later, in June 1965, Jack and Rachel learned that Jackie Jr. was on his way to Vietnam. The southeast Asian country was torn by a civil war between a pro-communist government in the North and an anti-communist government in the South. The US government supported the anti-communist forces, and by the end of 1965, it had sent more than 184,000 troops to Vietnam.

On November 19, 1965, Private First-Class Robinson and his platoon came under fierce assault. Bombs exploded all around them, and shrapnel flew everywhere.

A piece of hot metal struck Jackie in the hip. He cried out in pain, but he was still alive, still able to move.

Two friends next to him were badly wounded, and Jackie somehow managed to drag one of them out of the heat of battle. Both friends eventually died.

"We're very fortunate that our son was spared," Jack told reporters. "We feel deeply for the parents of our boy's slain fellow soldiers."

In an interview with the Associated Negro Press, Jack also said it was "very wrong" for US protesters to side with the communists in North Vietnam and criticize US soldiers.

Jack believed that "people with anti-war beliefs have every right to express themselves," but he wished that street protesters would do something more constructive, like fighting for civil rights.

Dr. King entered the public fray after he saw a wrenching photograph of a Vietnamese child killed by the US military. On April 4, 1967, he criticized US involvement in the war during a speech at Riverside Baptist Church in New York City.

Speaking somberly, he depicted the US government as an enemy of poor people. Money spent on killing poor Vietnamese people would better be spent on eliminating poverty, he said. He also observed that the war was racist because Black men served and died in combat in far greater percentages than white men did.

Dr. King speaking at an antiwar rally in New York City on April 15, 1967

Declaring the war unjust, King encouraged young men to refuse military service and demanded that the government declare a ceasefire and end all bombing campaigns.

The Riverside audience gave King a standing ovation, but his comments provoked criticism from across the country. Jack was among the vocal critics, and he used his newspaper column to publish an "open letter."

Jack criticized his friend for failing to see that a ceasefire would give North Vietnam time to rebuild resources for killing more US troops. He also charged King with being "unfair" for blaming only the United States.

Shortly later, Dr. King telephoned Jack in the quiet of an evening.

As Jack recounted it, "Before the rich, deep voice identified the caller, I knew that he was my dear friend, Dr. Martin Luther King, Jr."

The two talked openly and frankly about Jack's concerns, and while Jack said King's replies were "brilliant," he did not find them compelling enough to change all his opinions about the war.

But Jack was very grateful for the call, and he later spoke of his deep respect for King. "He is still my leader—a man to whose defense I would come at any time he might need me. That is a personal commitment and public pledge."

In the fall of 1967, heavyweight boxing champion Muhammad Ali, a member of the Nation of Islam, was convicted for refusing to submit to the military draft.

Defending his position, Ali said: "You want me to do what the white man says and go fight a war against some people I don't know nothing about—get some freedom for some other people when my own people can't get theirs here?"

Jack supported Ali amid a torrent of criticism descending on the boxer.

Jack admired Muhammad Ali's boxing skills, and he defended the boxing champion's right to speak out against the Vietnam War.

"In my view, [Ali] has demonstrated that he is fighting for a principle," Jack said. "While I cannot agree with it, I respect him sincerely."

Jack also applauded Ali for his apparent willingness to go to jail for refusing to be drafted.

"He was willing and prepared to make the challenge [against the draft] out of his deeply rooted convictions. And he is ready to accept the consequences. This is his heroism—and I believe it to be genuine."

About a week after defending Ali, Jack reiterated his support for increasing US involvement in the war.

"I am convinced that we must deal from a position of strength," Jack explained. "I have found this to be a good policy in athletics and I think it is probably the best policy in war."

Jack at the funeral of his good friend Dr. Martin Luther King Jr.

TWENTY-FIVE

REFUSING TO FLY THE FLAG

O n April 4, 1968, Martin Luther King Jr. stepped onto the balcony of his room at the Lorraine Motel in Memphis, Tennessee, to check the weather. He had come to the city to help sanitation workers protest for better working conditions.

As he stood alone, shots rang out. King's colleagues rushed outside and saw their leader lying on the cement. Reverend Ralph Abernathy, King's best friend, bent down, gently patted his mentor's cheeks, and told him everything would be okay.

King soon died, killed by an assassin's bullet.

As news of the murder spread, Black people lashed out in frustration and anger. Riots erupted in more than a hundred cities.

Jack was crushed, and in the days ahead, he praised his beloved friend as "the greatest leader of the twentieth century."

Jack channeled his grief into politics. Two months after Dr. King's death, he criticized Richard Nixon, the leading Republican candidate for president, for ignoring Black voters and civil rights.

"He has a right to feel that way," Jack said. "No one ever said bigotry was illegal. As for me, I have my right to remember that I am black and American before I am Republican. As such, I will never vote for Mr. Nixon."

When the Republican National Convention later nominated Nixon for the presidency, Jack said, "The Republican Party has told the black man to go to hell. I offer them a similar invitation."

As he turned away from the Republicans, Jack did something surprising: he expressed his support for the Black Panthers, a favorite Republican target. It was a remarkable move that showed he was inching closer to embracing the legacy of Malcolm X.

THE BLACK PANTHER PARTY

In October 1966, Bobby Seale and Huey Newton, two Black students at Merritt Junior College in Oakland, California, drafted a ten-point document that served as the manifesto for a new civil rights organization—the Black Panther Party for Self-Defense. The now-historic document demanded full employment, decent housing, and a high-quality education for Black people. It also called for an immediate end to police brutality. Although the Black Panthers are still known primarily for their willingness to use physical force for self-defense, most of their everyday work focused on social welfare programs that helped Black people gain access to health care, education, transportation, clothing, and food. Perhaps their most successful work was running a program that provided free breakfast for children.

The Black Panthers created free health clinics because of discrimination against poor Black people in hospitals and private doctors' offices.

On August 21, 1968, three Black Panthers were arrested for assaulting a police officer. Two weeks later, at a court hearing in Brooklyn, about 150 white men—including off-duty police officers—stormed the courthouse and used their fists, boots, and blackjacks to pummel ten Black Panthers and two white allies.

Several victims required hospitalization, and no arrests were made in the aftermath of the violent assaults.

Long angered by police brutality, Jack decided to visit with the Panthers at their headquarters in Brooklyn. Before speaking with them privately, he held a press conference where he mounted a spirited defense of the all-Black organization.

"Improper reporting has determined that they are a militant group while the fact is that they are seeking peace," he said.

Their goals were like those of other civil rights groups, he added. "The Black Panthers seek self-determination, protection of the Black community, decent housing and employment, and express opposition to police abuse."

Addressing the courthouse attack, he said: "They [the Panthers] had every reason to be violent after that kind of violence." The white attackers, including police officers, "should have been arrested then and there."

Jack also criticized police officers who were "trigger-happy" — inclined to shoot Black people first and talk later.

Meanwhile, numerous white politicians, including Richard Nixon, called for "law and order" when talking about Black communities that were revolting against police brutality.

Jack detested the phrase and understood it to mean that Nixon and other conservative politicians opposed civil rights and supported white police officers over Black people demanding safety and justice.

"If we expect Law and Order from Blacks, isn't it logical to expect Law and Order from whites?" Jack asked in a letter to a newspaper editor. If white leaders are so insistent on "law and order," they should immediately arrest and punish the white people responsible for brutalizing the Black Panthers, he said.

Jack's frustration with calls for "law and order" came to the fore when *The New York Times* interviewed him for an article about the US flag and Independence Day.

"I wouldn't fly the flag on the Fourth of July or any other day," Jack said, explaining that he saw the increasingly popular displaying of the flag as a sign of white opposition to civil rights.

The flag, he said, had become "captive" to those who, like Nixon and his supporters, scoffed at ongoing demands for Black justice.

Jack's wariness of patriotic symbols was not fleeting. He later wrote: "I cannot stand and sing the national anthem. I cannot salute the flag; I know that I am a black man in a white world."

While Nixon called for "law and order," Jack had his own "dangerous confrontation with a white police officer."

The fight broke out as Jack was walking into the Apollo Theater in Harlem for a visit with friends. As he told it,

> On my way into the lobby, an officer, a plainclothesman, accosted me. He asked me roughly where I was going, and I asked what the hell business it was of his. He grabbed me and spectators passing by told me later that he had pulled out his gun. I was so angry at his grabbing me and so busy telling him he'd better get his hands off me that I didn't remember seeing the gun. By this time people had started crowding around, excitedly telling him my name, and he backed off.

Jack escaped without physical harm, and he believed that the spectators, and his famous name, had saved him.

"Thinking over that incident, it horrifies me to realize what might have happened if I had been just another citizen of Harlem," he said.

"It shouldn't be necessary to be named Jackie Robinson to keep from getting brutalized" by white police officers.

By this point, Jack was struggling with health issues. In at the latest the summer of 1957, if not earlier, he had learned that he suffered from diabetes. He took insulin by injection and reduced sugar in his diet, but through the years, the disease advanced, damaging his eyes, legs, and heart. In 1969, he had a mild heart attack, and the following year, he had two strokes that left him uneasy on his feet and virtually blind. Doctors treated his advanced diabetes, but it had ravaged his body so much that they now discussed the possibility of amputating his leg.

Jack was deeply concerned about his rapidly failing health, but he would first have to face a death worse than his own.

TWENTY-SIX

HEADING HOME

Jack and Rachel lean on each other at the funeral for Jackie Jr.

On June 17, 1971, Jackie Jr. was behind the wheel of his brother David's sporty MG convertible. It was about 2:00 A.M., and he had just finished counseling kids in New York City about drug abuse.

Three years earlier, Jackie had been arrested for possessing illegal drugs. After facing another arrest, he stopped taking drugs and turned his life around with the help of Daytop Rehabilitation Program in New York. He was so successful that Daytop had hired him as a counselor to help other young addicts.

Driving home, Jackie lost control of the car, smashing it into a fence and an abutment. His injuries were severe, and he soon died.

Jack could not bring himself to identify his son's body at the morgue. "I had gone weak all over," he later wrote. "I knew that I couldn't go to that hospital or morgue or whatever and look at my dead son's body."

But Jack could not escape sharing the horrible news with Rachel, who was away at a conference, so he and Sharon drove to Holyoke, Massachusetts, while eighteen-year-old David went to identify his brother's body.

Rachel collapsed upon hearing about Jackie. Back home, she bolted from the car and ran aimlessly around their yard, screaming from the depths of pain that only she knew.

Jack, too, wept openly.

At the time of his death, Jackie Jr. had been organizing an "Afternoon of Jazz" to benefit Daytop. It was initially scheduled for early July, about a week after the accident, and Jack and Rachel decided to host the event despite their intense personal pain.

More than three thousand people turned out to honor Jackie Jr. and his antidrug work. The concert featured world-famous musicians—Roberta Flack, Herbie Mann, Dave Brubeck, and Dr. Billy Taylor—and raised about $40,000 for Daytop. The Robinsons were grateful—and heartbroken.

The year ahead would be emotionally draining for the entire family, but there would also be good news to celebrate.

A year after Jackie Jr.'s death, Peter O'Malley, president of the Los Angeles Dodgers, invited Jack to an "Old Timers' Day," where his famous number would be retired from team use.

Jack accepted the invitation, and on June 4, 1972, he walked onto the field at Dodger Stadium in Los Angeles. As the crowd erupted in cheers, fans must have been surprised to see that their hero had become an elderly man who had trouble seeing and walking.

"This is truly one of the greatest moments in my life," Jack told the hushed crowd.

Jack kept busy as his health deteriorated, and in August 1972, he announced that his new company, the Jackie Robinson Construction Corporation, had plans to build a large apartment complex for low- and moderate-income people in a primarily Black section of Brooklyn.

When explaining the project, Jack said, "I am grieved at the lack of decent housing for the young and the old. How do we expect to raise a child with decent standards and principles in all the filth he has to see, smell, and walk through every day of his life?"

Around this same time, MLB commissioner Bowie Kuhn telephoned Jack and invited him to throw out the first ball at one of the upcoming games of the 1972 World Series. The occasion would mark the twenty-fifth anniversary of his historic debut with the Brooklyn Dodgers.

Jack declined, citing his disappointment that there were still no Black managers in MLB. But when Kuhn told him that the event would also honor Jackie Jr. and Daytop, Jack accepted the invitation.

On October 15, Jack threw the ceremonial first pitch at the second game of the World Series. He was unsteady on his feet and virtually blind from diabetes, but with his family next to him, and a national viewing audience of sixty million before him, he sounded as strong and defiant as ever in a short speech.

"I am extremely proud and pleased to be here this afternoon," he said, "but must admit I'm going to be tremendously more pleased and more proud when I look at the third base coaching line one day and see a black face managing baseball."

No matter how sick he was, Jack continued to fight for Black justice.

Rachel woke up early on October 24, 1972.

After getting dressed, she went to the kitchen to make breakfast. It was standard fare, just like any other day. But then she

Jack throws out the ceremonial first pitch from the stands at the second game of the 1972 World Series. Son David, to his right, and MLB commissioner Bowie Kuhn, to his left, stand with him for the celebration.

saw Jack running down the hallway toward her. He wasn't yet dressed.

"So I ran out of the kitchen to meet him because I knew something was very wrong," she remembered. "And he put his arms around me and said, 'I love you.' And he just sank to the floor."

Felled by a heart attack, ravaged by diabetes, Jack Roosevelt Robinson died at 7:10 A.M.

More than 2,500 people—athletes, civil rights activists, jazz musicians, politicians, and other celebrities—attended the funeral at Riverside Baptist Church in New York City. Rachel asked for two-thirds of the seats to remain open for everyday citizens. She also insisted, because of Jack's love for children, that a section be reserved for the young ones.

Reverend Jesse Jackson delivered the eulogy. Jack had thought the

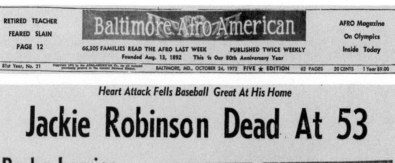

RETIRED TEACHER
FEARED SLAIN
PAGE 12

Baltimore Afro-American

AFRO Magazine
On Olympics
Inside Today

66,305 FAMILIES READ THE AFRO LAST WEEK   PUBLISHED TWICE WEEKLY
Founded Aug. 13, 1892   This is Our 80th Anniversary Year

81st Year, No. 21   Copyright 1972 by the AFRO-AMERICAN Co. for all material previously printed in the current National Edition.   BALTIMORE, MD., OCTOBER 24, 1972 FIVE ★ EDITION   62 PAGES   20 CENTS   1 Year $9.00

Heart Attack Fells Baseball Great At His Home

Jackie Robinson Dead At 53

Broke barrier in major league

STAMFORD. Conn., (UPI) — Jackie Robinson, who broke the major league color barrier in 1947 and went on to become one of baseball's brightest stars, died at home shortly before 6 a.m. this morning (Tuesday.) He was 53.

Robinson, whose brilliant 10-year career was capped by his election to the Hall of Fame in 1962, became a national celebrity when he joined the Brooklyn Dodgers. He shrugged off threats to his life and ignored the jibes of both teammates and opponents to be named Rookie of the Year in 1947. He led the Dodgers to the National League pennant that year.

But in recent years his luck seemed to sour. The distinguished, silver-haired man lost his oldest son, Jackie, Jr.—an admitted drug addict—in an auto accident. And late this summer, Robinson disclosed that his eyesight was failing.

* * *

Robinson was born in Cairo, Ga., on Jan. 31, 1919, and his family moved to Pasadena, Calif., when he was an infant. He went on to become a top scholar at UCLA, where he starred in football, basketball, baseball and track. He played professional football before joining the Kansas City

When Robinson joined the Dodgers in 1947, Rickey told him:

"I want a man with guts enough not to fight back."

"Replied Robinson: "Mr.

(Continued on Page 6)

Jackie's last statement 9 days ago

By SAM LACY

Jackie Robinson's last public utterance was made only nine days before his death Tuesday morning of a heart attack. It was his promise to be happy with baseball "only when I can look at the third base coaching box and see a black manager there."

The statement was made on national television at the high point of major league baseball's tribute to him as the first black player in the game. It was typical of the man. Throughout his career as athlete, business executive, politician, and humanitarian, Jackie nevever wavered from the determination to improve the lot

JACKIE ROBINSON, the baseball great, was signed up as a first with the Brooklyn Dodgers Oct. 24, 1945, 27 years before the date of his death.

An excerpt from the front-page article in the Baltimore Afro-American
(October 24, 1972)

world of Jackson and had recently agreed to serve as vice president of his new civil rights organization—People United to Save Humanity (Operation PUSH).

"When Jackie took the field, something reminded us of our birthright to be free," Jackson said in his eulogy. A church choir sang a tribute that included a song titled "If I Can Help Somebody."

The funeral procession weaved through Harlem and past Freedom National Bank before heading to Brooklyn and into Cypress Hills Cemetery. Hundreds of people lined the streets to pay their respects to the fallen hero. Jack was laid next to Jackie Jr.

Inscribed on his tombstone were words he had spoken and acted on: "A life is not important except in the impact it has on others."

Even in death, Jack inspires.

Rachel, center, is assisted by her son David, to her right, and Reverend Jesse Jackson, to her left, after the funeral service for Jack at Riverside Baptist Church in New York City.

ACKNOWLEDGMENTS

What a team!

Thanks to our wonderful agents, John Rudolph and Joan Brookbank, for believing in us and refining our pitch to Farrar, Straus, and Giroux Books for Young Readers.

Executive editor Wesley Adams took a big swing and connected, driving the ball deep toward the home-run fence. We could not be more grateful than we are for his brilliant editing and unfailing collegiality. If there's ever a Hall of Fame for book editors, Wes deserves entry in his first year of eligibility.

Our appreciation extends to editorial assistant Hannah Miller and production editor Ilana Worrell for expertly ensuring that we touched the bases.

The Macmillan Children's Publishing Group, especially Morgan Rath, Teresa Ferraiolo, and Mary Van Akin, cheered early on. Many thanks for their remarkable efforts to pack the stadium. We also applaud all the players in the dugout — the designers, copyeditors, proofreaders, production managers, as well as the librarians, archivists, newspaper staffs, and photographers.

Our family and friends deserve our big thanks for pumping their fists from deep in the cheap seats. Yohuru thanks his research assistants, Brynn Kimel and Ella Williams, for their outstanding assistance, and his partner, Alexandra Alves, for reading countless drafts and sharing her great passion and enthusiasm for young readers. Mike thanks Karin Long, Nate Long, Jackson Long, Elda Hricko, Sharon Herr, Bob Long, and Shea Tuttle.

Finally, we thank our young readers for their interest in learning about the life and legacy of Jack Roosevelt Robinson. May each of you continue his fight for first-class citizenship for all people.

EXTRA-INNING FACTS

Here are some fascinating facts not mentioned in our story.

During his childhood and young adulthood in Pasadena, Jack

- suffered from a life-threatening case of diphtheria.
- was a regular at the local library until he focused on sports.
- won the pentathlon award in elementary school.
- participated in a citywide marble-shooting championship.
- sang in the glee club.
- sold hot dogs at the Rose Bowl.
- weighed 135 pounds when he started playing high school football.
- played mixed tennis doubles with an ambidextrous partner, Eleanor Peters.

During his junior college and university years, he

- encouraged PJC's Black students to stop sitting in the balcony during assemblies.
- loved softball.
- led the Pasadena Sox, an interracial baseball team sponsored by the Chicago White Sox, to victory in the Southern California amateur baseball championships.

- missed the extra-point kick after running for a ninety-two-yard touchdown for PJC's football team.
- taught Black students every Sunday at Scott Methodist Church.
- probably would have participated in the long jump at the 1940 Olympics if they had not been canceled because of the war in Europe.

In the US Army, he

- was part of the nation's first integrated Officer Candidate School.
- wore the uniform of a cavalry officer before commanding a tank battalion.
- won the Army's championship table-tennis match.

During his professional baseball career, he

- played part of a season with the Los Angeles Reds, a professional basketball team.
- worked as a counselor and coach at the Harlem YMCA.
- became the first Black American to appear on the cover of *Life* magazine.
- starred as himself in a film titled *The Jackie Robinson Story*.
- opened the Jackie Robinson Store, specializing in men's clothing, in Harlem.
- became editor of *Our Sports*, a monthly magazine for Black people.
- visited sick children in hospitals.
- met and inspired Wilma Rudolph, who said Jack was her "first black hero."
- was the first Black player ejected from a game in Japan.

- became director of community activities, with a focus on juvenile delinquency, for NBC television stations in New York City.
- faced discrimination when trying to buy property in Connecticut.
- was caught stealing home twelve times.
- stole home nineteen times.
- expressed interest in becoming the first Black manager in MLB.

After baseball, he

- successfully lobbied the Professional Golfers Association to grant membership to its first Black player, Charlie Sifford.
- was picketed by Black nationalists, including followers of Malcolm X, in Harlem after he opposed their efforts to stop the sale of a local restaurant to a white man.
- wrote a nationally syndicated column for the *New York Amsterdam News.*
- was criticized by Jesse Owens for speaking to Birmingham's civil rights activists in 1963.
- criticized Black athletes, including Frank Robinson, for not being active in the Black civil rights movement.
- played in charity golf tournaments with Black tennis star Althea Gibson.
- became the first Black analyst for MLB games on ABC-TV Sports.
- was denied membership in the High Ridge Country Club in Stamford.
- tried but failed to build an interracial country club.
- became manager of the Brooklyn Dodgers football team in the Continental Football League.

- played Santa Claus for poor children in New Jersey.
- delivered food to a Brooklyn pantry for poor people.
- spoke at antidrug abuse events with Jackie Jr.
- loved to golf.
- enjoyed betting on horses.

After Jack died, Rachel

- resigned from her work in psychiatric nursing at Yale University.
- became president of the Jackie Robinson Construction Corporation.
- supervised the construction of housing for low- to moderate-income residents.
- founded and served as president of the Jackie Robinson Management Company, a real estate management and training company.
- founded and served as president of the Jackie Robinson Foundation, which continues to provide scholarships to college and university students.
- helped found the Jackie Robinson Museum.

After Jack's death

- he was awarded the Presidential Medal of Freedom.
- Major League Baseball retired his number.
- his image appeared on a US postage stamp and on gold and silver coins produced by the US Mint.
- he was awarded the Congressional Gold Medal.
- he was featured in an award-winning film (*42*), an award-winning documentary (*Jackie Robinson*), and numerous books for people of all ages.

THINGS TO THINK ABOUT

- Was Jack the greatest athlete in US history?
- How would his life have been different if he had not been an exceptional athlete?
- If he were alive today, who would his favorite athlete be?
- How would Jack's life have been different if Mallie had decided to stay in Georgia?
- If he were alive today, would he support the Black Lives Matter movement?
- Would he stand for the national anthem at sporting events?
- What do you think about athletes who are also activists for social justice?
- Is there an issue that you feel strongly about and would protest for?
- How did Jack demonstrate teamwork and cooperation? Why are these important traits?
- How did he deal with setbacks? What can we learn from his approach?
- Did Jack do anything that shocked or surprised you?
- If you could ask him one question, what would it be?

TIMELINE

YEAR EVENT

YEAR	EVENT
1919	Born in Cairo, Georgia.
1920	Migrates to Pasadena, California, at age sixteen months with mother Mallie Robinson and siblings Edgar (ten), Frank (nine), Mack (six), and Willa Mae (four).
1922	Moves with the family to 121 Pepper Street.
1937	Graduates from John Muir Technical High School.
1937–1939	Attends Pasadena Junior College.
1939–1941	Attends the University of California at Los Angeles, earning letters in four varsity sports.
1940	Meets Rachel Isum.
1941	Works for the National Youth Administration.
	Plays for the Honolulu Bears.
1942	Plays for the Los Angeles Bulldogs.
	Is drafted into the US Army.
1943	Becomes a second lieutenant.
1944	Refuses to move to the back of a bus and is court-martialed, acquitted, and honorably discharged.

1945   Teaches and coaches at Samuel Huston College.

Plays for the Kansas City Monarchs.

Has a "tryout" with the Boston Red Sox.

Meets Branch Rickey.

1946   Marries Rachel Isum.

Plays for the Montreal Royals.

Helps the Royals win the Junior World Series.

Son Jackie Jr. is born.

1947   Debuts with the Brooklyn Dodgers on April 15, cracking the color barrier in Major League Baseball.

Wins Rookie of the Year award.

1949   Testifies before the House Un-American Activities Committee.

Named the National League's Most Valuable Player.

1950   Daughter Sharon is born.

Stars in the *The Jackie Robinson Story*.

1952   Son David is born.

1955   Helps the Dodgers win the World Series.

1956   Receives the NAACP's Spingarn Medal.

Is traded to the New York Giants.

Retires before playing for his new team.

1957   Becomes vice president of personnel at Chock Full o'Nuts.

Leads the NAACP's Freedom Fund Drive.

Receives honorary degree of doctor of laws from Howard University.

1958   Marches in the Youth March for Integrated Schools.

1959   Marches in the Second Youth March for Integrated Schools.

Becomes a *New York Post* columnist.

1960 Campaigns for Republican presidential candidate
Richard Nixon.

1961 Is elected to the National Baseball Hall of Fame.

1962 Travels to the Albany Movement led by Dr. King.

Raises funds for three Black churches torched by
segregationists.

Becomes a columnist for the *New York Amsterdam
News*.

1963 Travels to the Birmingham Movement led by Dr. King.

Gives a welcome speech at the March on Washington
for Jobs and Freedom.

Criticizes Malcolm X.

1964 Marches against Republican presidential candidate
Barry Goldwater.

1965 Cofounds Freedom National Bank in Harlem.

Jackie Jr. is wounded in the Vietnam War.

1966 Opposes the Black Power movement.

1967 Criticizes Dr. King's speech against US involvement in
the Vietnam War.

1968 Supports the Black Panthers in their fight against police
brutality.

Opposes Richard Nixon as the Republican presidential
candidate.

1969 Tells the *New York Times* he refuses to fly the US flag.

1970 With Jackie Jr., gives antidrug talks in schools.

Co-founds the Jackie Robinson Construction Corporation.

1971 Jackie Jr. dies.

1972 Number 42 is retired by the Los Angeles Dodgers.

Dies of a heart attack and complications from diabetes.

NOTES

ONE: Taking the Freedom Train

3 "Where's the backbones?" and "Where's the neckbones?": No author, "Mrs. Robinson's Notes," no date, Papers of Jackie Robinson [JRP], box 15, Library of Congress, Washington, DC. This is an unpublished transcript from an interview of Mallie Robinson for Carl T. Rowan with Jackie Robinson, *Wait Till Next Year: The Life Story of Jackie Robinson* (New York: Random House, 1960). This interview is the main source for our description of Mallie's time on the farm and her decision to leave.

3 "Slavery's over!": "Mrs. Robinson's Notes," no date.

4 "I sure like you": "Mrs. Robinson's Notes," no date.

4 "Let's prove to the world": "Mrs. Robinson's Notes," no date.

4 "Let's try and farm": "Mrs. Robinson's Notes," no date.

5 "And every time we got": "Mrs. Robinson's Notes," no date.

6 "As a race": Christopher Klein, "How Teddy Roosevelt's Belief in a Racial Hierarchy Shaped His Policies," history.com, August 11, 2020, history.com/news/teddy-roosevelt-race-imperialism-national-parks.

7 "about the sassiest nigger": "Mrs. Robinson's Notes," no date.

9 "Freedom Train": Rachel Robinson with Lee Daniels, *Jackie Robinson: An Intimate Portrait* (New York: Harry N. Abrams, 1996), 14.

TWO: Throwing Stones

11   "the most beautiful sight": "Mrs. Robinson's Notes," no date.

12   "They left on their own": "Great Migration: The African-American Exodus North," npr.org, September 13, 2010, npr.org/templates/story/story.php?storyId=129827444.

13   "easy terms": "11-ROOM HOUSE, JUST PAINTED," advertisement, *Pasadena Evening Post*, March 21, 1921.

13   "I'm afraid she'll be": "Mrs. Robinson's Notes," no date.

14   "Nigger! Nigger! Nigger!," "nothing but a cracker," and "Soda cracker's": Rowan and Robinson, *Wait Till Next Year*, 25.

15   "Robinson Crusoe": Arnold Rampersad, *Jackie Robinson: A Biography* (New York: Alfred A. Knopf, 1997), 24.

16   "We would get to school": Rampersad, *Jackie Robinson*, 26.

THREE: Stoking the Fire

18   "A cold wind": "Fast Times," *Pasadena Post*, May 7, 1930.

18   in quotation marks, as "Jackie": "Team Claims Record," *Pasadena Post*, October 21, 1930.

18   "Both teams were probably": "Jefferson Captures City League Title," *Pasadena Post*, February 7, 1931.

20   "Gardener": Rampersad, *Jackie Robinson*, 27.

20   "I could only think" and "He had no right": Jackie Robinson and Alfred Duckett, *I Never Had It Made* (Hopewell, NJ: Ecco Press, 1995), 4.

21   "venerable residence" and "occupied by": "Landmark Is Periled by Flames," *Pasadena Post*, August 19, 1933. The property was a "landmark" because it was "one of the oldest residences on the northside," an area that small ranches once occupied.

21   "the Castle": Rampersad, *Jackie Robinson*, 22–23.

22   "Through some miracle" and "I remember I cried": Rampersad, *Jackie Robinson*, 33.

23   "pale": "Mrs. Robinson's Notes," no date.

FOUR: Tarring Jim Crow

26   shouting about "niggers": Rowan and Robinson, *Wait Till Next Year*, 31.

26   "escorted to jail": Rampersad, *Jackie Robinson*, 34.

26   "Our gang": Robinson and Duckett, *I Never Had It Made*, 6.

26   "We threw dirt clods": Robinson and Duckett, *I Never Had It Made*, 6.

27   "All the time": Robinson and Duckett, *I Never Had It Made*, 6–7.

30   "How we going" and "I don't care": "Mrs. Robinson's Notes," no date.

FIVE: Snatching Sacks

34   "the champion sack snatcher" and "Jack 'Smoky' Robinson": "Base Steal-
     ing Profitable," *Pomona Progress Bulletin*, April 10, 1936.

34   "You [toe] the line" and "Then you jump": Rampersad, *Jackie Robinson*, 36.

34   "If there was one person": David Falkner, *Great Time Coming: The Life
     of Jackie Robinson from Baseball to Birmingham* (New York: Simon and
     Schuster, 1995), 35.

35   "colored flash": "Cards Beaten by Muir Tech in Cage Tilt," *Whittier News*,
     February 22, 1936.

35   "dusky sharpshooter": "Double Victory Scored By Terrier Fives," *Pasa-
     dena Post*, January 6, 1937.

35   "black lightning": "Muir Tech Wallops Covina Colts in Basketball,"
     Covina Argus, January 22, 1937.

35   "the best passer": "Pomona High Given Chance to Upset Classy Terriers in
     Local Armistice Clash," *Pomona Progress Bulletin*, November 10, 1936.

36   "piled on": "Foothill Honor to Glendale," *Pasadena Post*, November 22,
     1936.

37   "The game was rough": "Muir 'Blows Lead,' Loses to Whittier," *Pasadena
     Post*, February 4, 1937.

SIX: Banding with Black Bulldogs

39   "Coach Mallory laid": Rampersad, *Jackie Robinson*, 49.

40   "a dark-hued phantom," and "brilliant running and passing": Shavenau
     Glick, "Robinson Big Star of Game," *Pasadena Post*, November 25, 1937.

42   "nearly all the people": *Pasadena Post*, January 23, 1938, quoted in Rampersad, *Jackie Robinson*, 50; see also *Pasadena Chronicle* account in Rowan and Robinson, *Wait Till Next Year*, 36–37.

43   "considered the greatest college baseball player": Dave Meikeljohn, "Sport Static," *Pomona Progress Bulletin*, May 10, 1938.

43   "Geez, if that kid was white": Rampersad, *Jackie Robinson*, 55.

43   "The greatest football throng": George Garner, "Jack Robinson Leads Pasadena to Victory," *Chicago Defender*, November 5, 1938.

44   "We weren't allowed to stay": Falkner, *Great Time Coming*, 45.

SEVEN: Resisting Arrest

45   "before you are clubbed": "Brother of Jack Robinson Beaten by Pasadena Police," *California Eagle*, January 12, 1939.

46   "to promote equality": "NAACP: A Century in the Fight for Freedom: Founding and Early Years," loc.gov, no date, loc.gov/exhibits/naacp/founding-and-early-years.html.

47   "wickedly unorthodox style": Almena Davis, "Amazing Play of Robinson Steals Tennis Spotlight," *California Eagle*, July 6, 1939.

47   "I was very shaken up" and "It was hard": Robinson and Duckett, *I Never Had It Made*, 10.

48   "the biggest argument for": J. Cullen Fentress, "The Negro and the Major Leagues," *California Eagle*, August 7, 1939.

48   something derogatory about "niggers": Falkner, *Great Time Coming*, 47.

48   "But not Jack," "He just wouldn't": Rampersad, *Jackie Robinson*, 65.

48   "I found myself up against" and "I was scared": Rampersad, *Jackie Robinson*, 65.

49   "I got out of that trouble": Rampersad, *Jackie Robinson*, 66.

49   "the juiciest plum," "jittery jack rabbit," and "UCLA will boast": Frank Finch, "Jackie Robinson Enters UCLA," *Los Angeles Times*, February 17, 1939.

49   "All Jackie did": Paul Zimmerman, "Jackie Robinson Big Threat on UCLA Football Eleven," *Los Angeles Times*, August 27, 1939.

50   "Jackie 'Jumping Jive' Robinson": Chester L. Washington, Jr., "Sez Ches," *The Pittsburgh Courier*, September 23, 1939.

50 "a positive menace": "Robinson Showed the Boys Some Speed," *Los Angeles Daily News*, October 2, 1939.

50 "the Brown phantom": Herman Hill, "Kenny Washington 20–Montana 6!" *The Pittsburgh Courier*, October 28, 1939.

50 "Jackie the Jitterbug": Bob Hebert, "'Best in History' Bruins Due Today," *Los Angeles Daily News*, October 11, 1939.

50 "the halfback with wings on his feet": Lowell Redellings, "Robinson Sure to Get 'Go' Signal," *Hollywood Citizen-News*, October 27, 1939.

50 "the fastest man in college football": Lucius "Melancholy" Jones, "Slants on Sports," *Atlanta Daily World*, December 6, 1939.

50 "the greatest halfback in America": Paul Zimmerman, "Sport Post-Scripts," *Los Angeles Times*, October 22, 1939.

50 "You need mechanized cavalry": Paul Lowry, "Robinson Too Hard to Stop, Says Oliver," *Los Angeles Times*, October 29, 1939.

50 "may go on to hand Battler Jim Crow": J. Cullen Fentress, "Down in Front," *California Eagle*, December 28, 1939.

51 "black magic": Bob Ray, "The Sports X-Ray," *Los Angeles Times*, February 9, 1940.

51 "speedy dribbling dashes": "Robinson Tallies 23 Points but Bruins Lose," *Los Angeles Daily News*, January 13, 1940.

51 "eagle eye": "Jack Robinson Gives UCLA Win Over Cal 'Big Brothers' 34–32," *Whittier News*, February 5, 1940.

51 "body control and judgment": Dick Hyland, "Behind the Line," *Los Angeles Times*, March 2, 1940.

51 "the best basketball player": Hyland, "Behind the Line," March 2, 1940.

51 "player of the year": Cited in Wendell Smith, "Smitty's Sport Spurts," *The Pittsburgh Courier*, March 9, 1940.

51 "had it not been": Ned Cronin, "Second Guess," *Los Angeles Daily News*, February 13, 1940.

52 "There's nothing major leaguish": "Rube" Samuelsen, "Sport Volleys," *Pasadena Post*, May 18, 1940.

53 "was UCLA's first": "UCLA to Induct Eight New Members into Athletic Hall of Fame," uclabruins.com, September 22, 2009, uclabruins.com /news/2009/9/22/207898058.

53 "Robinson was UCLA's": Houston Mitchell, "Greatest Sports Figures in L.A. History, No. 10: Jackie Robinson," latimesblogs.com, October 26, 2011, latimesblogs.latimes.com/sports_blog/2011/10/greatest-sports -figures-in-la-history-no-10-jackie-robinson.html.

53 "One of the greatest athletes": Robinson and Daniels, *Jackie Robinson*, 20.

EIGHT: Falling in Love

55 "I was the aggressor": *Jackie Robinson*, episode 1, directed by Ken Burns, Sarah Burns, and David McMahon, produced by Florentine Films and WETA in Washington, DC, in association with Major League Baseball, 2016.

56 "He was big": Gary Libman, "Rachel Robinson's Homecoming," *Los Angeles Times*, September 2, 1987.

56 "He was clearly comfortable": "Interview with Rachel Robinson," scholastic.com, no date, scholastic.com/teachers/articles/teaching-content /interview-rachel-robinson.

56 "Jack displayed his color": Libman, "Rachel Robinson's Homecoming," September 2, 1987.

56 "I was extremely shy" and "However, my impression": "Interview with Rachel Robinson."

56 "I was immediately attracted" and "When she left": Robinson and Duck- ett, *I Never Had It Made*, 10.

56 "There are few people": Robinson and Duckett, *I Never Had It Made*, 11.

57 "I was excited and happy": Rampersad, *Jackie Robinson*, 80.

57 "flagrant bit of prejudice": Rampersad, *Jackie Robinson*, 82.

58 "I was aghast" and "I tried": Rampersad, *Jackie Robinson*, 82.

58 "That Jackie Robinson": "Jackie Robinson Sensation of All-Star Game Before 98,200," *Afro-American*, September 6, 1941.

59 "We were determined": Jim Mendoza, "Jackie Robinson Broke Tackles on Hawaii's Gridiron," *Hawaii News Now*, April 16, 2013.

59 "was scared at first": "Mainland Sports Dope," *Honolulu Star-Bulletin*, January 20, 1942.

NINE: Fighting the Army

62   "unwritten law," "The matter is out," and "Personally": Herman Hill, "Jackie Robinson, Nate Moreland Barred at Camp," *The Pittsburgh Courier*, March 21, 1942.

62   "several White Sox players": "The Black Sportswriter," *Ebony*, October 1970, 60.

62   "I plan to work hard": "Army Induction Officer Here Swears in His Last Recruits," *Los Angeles Times*, April 4, 1942.

63   overall character as "excellent": Rampersad, *Jackie Robinson*, 91.

63   "I'll break up the team": Rampersad, *Jackie Robinson*, 91.

64   "The present defense program": Michael G. Long, ed., *Marshalling Justice: The Early Civil Rights Letters of Thurgood Marshall* (New York: Amistad, 2011), 75.

64   "In accordance with": Long, *Marshalling Justice*, 78.

65   "Lieutenant, let me put it": Rowan and Robinson, *Wait Till Next Year*, 73.

65   "Pure rage took over": Robinson and Duckett, *I Never Had It Made*, 14. All sentences in this paragraph come from this source.

66   "[Renegar] tells me": "Sworn Statement of 2nd Lt. Jack R. Robinson, Company B, 761st Tank Battalion, Camp Hood, Texas, 7 July 1944," in Michael Lee Lanning, *The Court-Martial of Jackie Robinson* (Lanham, MD: Stackpole Books, 2020), 174.

66   "When he got to the bus station": Lanning, *The Court-Martial of Jackie Robinson*, 174. All sentences in this paragraph come from this source.

66   referred to him as a "nigger" and "I told him": Lanning, *The Court-Martial of Jackie Robinson*, 175.

66   "Lt. Robinson's attitude": Lanning, *The Court-Martial of Jackie Robinson*, 57.

68   "vile, obscene, and abusive language": Lanning, *The Court-Martial of Jackie Robinson*, 54.

68   "My Grandmother gave me": "Court-Martial Transcript," in Lanning, *The Court-Martial of Jackie Robinson*, 241–42. All sentences in this explanation come from this source.

68 "inactive status": Jack R. Robinson, letter to Adjutant General, War Department, September 1944, in Lanning, *The Court-Martial of Jackie Robinson*, 214.

68 "by reason of physical disqualification": Rampersad, *Jackie Robinson*, 111.

TEN: Fueling the Negro Leagues

72 "There was very little money": Robinson and Duckett, *I Never Had It Made*, 69.

72 "Well, Jackie, I didn't even know," "Yeah," and "I play": Jake Harris, "Jackie Robinson Once Coached Basketball at Austin College," *Austin American-Statesman*, October 12, 2016.

73 "a pretty miserable way": Robinson and Duckett, *I Never Had It Made*, 24.

74 "jump between cities": Falkner, *Great Time Coming*, 93.

74 "This fatiguing travel": Robinson and Duckett, *I Never Had It Made*, 24.

75 "Boy, where are you going?" and "I'm going": Bill Ladson, "Jackie's MLB Success Was Negro Leagues' Loss," MLB.com, August 27, 2020, mlb.com /news/jackie-robinson-success-decline-of-negro-leagues.

76 "What a ballplayer!": Rampersad, *Jackie Robinson*, 120.

76 "Ace of [the] Monarchs" and "studded with many": "Jackie Robinson Ace of Monarchs," *Wilmington Morning News*, June 21, 1945.

76 "The sensational infielder": Bill Burk, "Sports Shorts," *The Delaware County Daily Times*, July 14, 1945.

ELEVEN: Staring at Rickey

77 "Hey, Robinson": Clyde Sukeforth as told to Donald Honig, "Oh, They Were a Pair," in *The Jackie Robinson Reader*, ed. Jules Tygiel (New York: Dutton, 1997), 67.

77 "I see": Rowan and Robinson, *Wait Till Next Year*, 113.

77 "Who's the white fellow": Jackie Robinson as told to Wendell Smith, *Jackie Robinson: My Own Story* (New York: Greenburg, 1948), 16.

78 "He told me to come out," "Why is Mr. Rickey interested," "He *also* said," and "Jack, this could be": Sukeforth and Honig, "Oh, They Were a Pair," 68.

79 "Oh, they were a pair": Sukeforth and Honig, "Oh, They Were a Pair," 69.

79 "You were brought here": Rampersad, *Jackie Robinson*, 126.

80 "I was thrilled": Robinson and Duckett, *I Never Had It Made*, 31.

80 "I want to win the pennant," "Do you think you can?" "Jack waited," "Yes," and "I know you're a good": Rampersad, *Jackie Robinson*, 126.

81 "I was twenty-six years old," "Are you looking," and "Robinson, I'm looking": Robinson and Duckett, *I Never Had It Made*, 33.

82 "I didn't know how": Robinson and Duckett, *I Never Had It Made*, 34.

82 "had more kindness": Rampersad, *Jackie Robinson*, 111.

82 "It suddenly felt": Rampersad, *Jackie Robinson*, 134.

TWELVE: Crushing the Minors

84 "It was kind of horrendous": Tom Canavan, "Rachel Robinson Recalls Husband's Pioneering Game," *Los Angeles Times*, April 21, 1996.

84 "as if it were full": Rampersad, *Jackie Robinson*, 149.

84 "a Southern gentleman": Dink Carroll, "Playing the Field," *Montreal Gazette*, April 19, 1946.

84 "Do you really think?": Rampersad, *Jackie Robinson*, 142.

85 "too moist to grip": Jules Tygiel, *Baseball's Great Experiment: Jackie Robinson and His Legacy* (New York: Oxford University Press, 1983), 5.

87 "Hell": Canavan, "Rachel Robinson Recalls Husband's Pioneering Game," April 21, 1996.

87 "mad scene," "happy as a kid," and "The one thing that I cared about": "Robinson Paces Royals to 14–1 Win," *Montreal Gazette*, April 19, 1946.

87 "She wanted me to quit": "Jackie Robinson Sure to Be with 1947 Dodgers," *St. Joseph News Press*, September 16, 1946.

88 "Syracuse rode me harder": Robinson and Smith, *Jackie Robinson*, 106.

88 "some of the foulest names": Sean Kirst, "Syracuse Faces an Ugly Legacy from the Jackie Robinson Era," *Syracuse Post-Standard*, April 21, 1997.

89 "Most of us could not": Canavan, "Rachel Robinson Recalls Husband's Pioneering Game," April 21, 1996.

89 "He's a big-league ballplayer": Patrick Sauer, "The Year of Jackie Robinson's Mutual Love Affair with Montreal," Smithsonianmag.com, April 6, 2015, smithsonianmag.com/history/year-jackie-robinsons-mutual-love -affair-montreal-180954878.

THIRTEEN: Becoming Jackie Again

91 "The Brooklyn Dodgers today": Louis Effrat, "Of Skill and Courage," *The New York Times*, April 10, 1947.

91 "I know now that dreams": Jackie Robinson, "Jackie Robinson Says," *The Pittsburgh Courier*, April 19, 1947.

91 "I don't care if the guy": Rampersad, *Jackie Robinson*, 164.

92 "It is a peculiar sensation": W. E. Burghardt Du Bois, "Strivings of the Negro People," *The Atlantic*, August 1897, theatlantic.com/magazine /archive/1897/08/strivings-of-the-negro-people/305446.

94 "The first to play": John R. Husman, "Moses Fleetwood Walker, sabr.org, no date, sabr.org/bioproj/person/fleet-walker.

94 "Moses Fleetwood Walker remains": Richard Goldstein, "Overlooked: Moses Fleetwood Walker," nytimes.com, no date, nytimes.com/interactive /2019/obituaries/moses-fleetwood-walker-overlooked.html.

94 "the first African-American": John Harris, "Moses Fleetwood Walker Was the First African American to Play Pro Baseball, Six Decades Before Jackie Robinson," theundefeated.com, February 22, 2017, theundefeated.com/features/moses-fleetwood-walker-was-the-first -african-american-to-play-pro-baseball-six-decades-before-jackie -robinson.

95 "I looked for a locker": Robinson and Smith, *Jackie Robinson*, 126.

95 "I finally got dressed": Robinson and Smith, *Jackie Robinson*, 126.

FOURTEEN: Controlling His Temper

97 "Hey, nigger," "They're waiting for you," "We don't want you here," and "Go back": Rampersad, *Jackie Robinson*, 172.

98 "I was, after all": Robinson and Duckett, *I Never Had It Made*, 58.

98 "For one wild and rage-crazed": Robinson and Duckett, *I Never Had It Made*, 59.

99   "Listen, you yellow-bellied": Robinson and Duckett, *I Never Had It Made*, 60.

100   "And don't bring your team": Rampersad, *Jackie Robinson*, 175–176.

100   "having my picture taken": Robinson and Duckett, *I Never Had It Made*, 62.

100   "Jackie, you know": Jonathan Eig, *Opening Day: The Story of Jackie Robinson's First Season* (New York: Simon and Schuster, 2007), 105.

FIFTEEN: Straightening His Back

104   "unthinkable that American Negroes": Martin Duberman, *Paul Robeson: A Biography* (New York: Ballentine Books, 1990), 341–42.

104   "Rae and I remembered": Rowan and Robinson, *Wait Till Next Year*, 203.

105   he would be a "traitor": Robinson and Duckett, *I Never Had It Made*, 84.

105   "an expert on" and all other quotations from his testimony: Jackie Robinson, "Statement to House Un-American Activities Committee, July 19, 1949," in Thomas W. Zeiler, *Jackie Robinson and Race in America* (Boston: Bedford/St. Martin's, 2014), 111–15. Civil rights leader Lester Granger helped to draft the document. See also Eric Nusbaum, "The Story Behind Jackie Robinson's Moving Testimony Before the House Un-American Activities Committee," time.com, March 24, 2020, time.com/5808543/jackie-robinson-huac.

107   "Jackie Flays Bias": Rampersad, *Jackie Robinson*, 215.

107   "Paul Robeson should have": Rampersad, *Jackie Robinson*, 216.

SIXTEEN: Kicking Jackie

109   "Get the manager out" and "Are you wearing": Wendell Smith, "Wendell Smith's Sports Beat," *The Pittsburgh Courier*, July 8, 1950.

109   "to get personal" and "You're damned right": Sam Lacy, "From A to Z with Sam Lacy," *Afro-American*, July 8, 1950.

110   "You've got a swelled head": Smith, "Sports Beat," July 8, 1950.

111   "Fans Like the New," "Robinson started out," and "Robinson is showing": "Fans Like the New Jackie Robinson; So Does B. Rickey," *Los Angeles Sentinel*, July 6, 1950.

111 "That pitch was right down": "Umpire 'Goaded' Him, Says Robbie After Ejection," *Afro-American*, July 8, 1950.

111 "My ass": This exact quote appears nowhere in print, but it is implied in "Umpires Given Too Much Authority—Robinson," *The Pittsburgh Courier*, July 8, 1950, which reads, "Robinson's retort was slightly sharper than 'My neck.'"

112 accused Conlan of "goading" and "What does he have": "Umpire 'Goaded' Him, Says Robbie After Ejection," July 8, 1950.

112 "might have put out," "There's no question" and "You can bet": "Umpire Trouble Still Plaguing Jackie Robinson," *The Pittsburgh Courier*, July 15, 1950.

113 "I know it's wrong," "I hate to see," and "No promises": "'No Promises, But I'll Try,'" *The Pittsburgh Courier*, July 26, 1952.

114 "I threw it at him": Wendell Smith, "Wendell Smith's Sports Beat," *The Pittsburgh Courier*, September 8, 1956.

SEVENTEEN: Winning the World Series

116 "It's close": Hear commentary and see footage of the steal at "Jackie Robinson Steals Home," YouTube.com, April 2, 2009, youtube.com/watch?v=6XY-XshGhMU.

116 "A successful steal": Chauncey Durden, "The Sportview," *Richmond Times-Dispatch*, September 29, 1955.

116 "a steal of home like that" and "I was safe": "Two Runs by Collins Back Ford," *Richmond Times-Dispatch*, September 29, 1955.

116 "whether it was because": Robinson and Duckett, *I Never Had It Made*, 120.

118 "All Walter said": Gayle Talbot, "Sport Roundup," *Ventura County Star-Free Press*, April 7, 1955.

118 "insubordination such as seldom" and "No matter what": Talbot, "Sport Roundup," April 7, 1955.

119 Jack was "irritated," "a man goaded," and "desire": Jimmy Cannon, "No Dodger Fold," *Kansas City Star*, October 3, 1955.

119 "The real reason": Robert Rubino, "When Brooklyn Won It All, Jackie Robinson Sat," *Santa Rosa Press Democrat*, October 3, 2015.

119 "His hair is gray": Rampersad, *Jackie Robinson*, 285.

120 "With the world championship": Rampersad, *Jackie Robinson*, 285.

EIGHTEEN: Marching for Integrated Schools

123 "the highest or noblest achievement": "Awards: Spingarn Medal," NAACP
.org, no date, naacp.org/find-resources/scholarships-awards-internships
/awards.

124 "civic consciousness," and "citizen of democracy": "Citation for Jackie
Robinson, 41st Spingarn Medalist, December 8, 1956," in *By Popular
Demand: Jackie Robinson and Other Baseball Highlights, 1860s–1960s*,
loc.gov, no date, loc.gov/collections/jackie-robinson-baseball/articles
-and-essays/baseball-the-color-line-and-jackie-robinson/citation-for
-jackie-robinson.

124 "Today marks the high point": Samuel Haynes, "'High Point of My
Career'—Jackie of Spingarn Award," *Afro-American*, December 8, 1956.

125 "I left baseball": Jackie Robinson, Home Plate, *New York Amsterdam
News*, January 12, 1962.

126 "If my name was": Robinson and Duckett, *I Never Had It Made*, 126.

126 "There was a time" and "Then I realized": Rampersad, *Jackie Robinson*,
317.

127 "Why wait? Integrate!," "Two, four, six, eight!," and "Phooey on Faubus": Edward Peeks, "Students Rebuffed Trying to See Ike," *Washington
Afro-American*, October 25, 1958.

127 "You have demonstrated" and "I'm sorry": Peeks, "Students Rebuffed,"
October 25, 1958.

NINETEEN: Extinguishing Hatred

131 "I directed my 'fiery' temper" and "If I honestly": Jackie Robinson, Home
Plate, *New York Amsterdam News*, January 12, 1962.

131 "I just want to say": Jackie Robinson, Home Plate *New York Amsterdam
News*, February 3, 1962.

132 "a lifetime batting average" and "He became a living fulfillment": "It Was
Jackie Robinson's Week," *New York Amsterdam News*, July 28, 1962.

133 "The only hope": "It Was Jackie Robinson's Week," July 28, 1962.

133   "He has the right": Martin Luther King Jr., "Hall of Famer," *New York Amsterdam News*, August 4, 1962.

133   "the funeral of a church": Jackie Robinson, Home Plate, *New York Amsterdam News*, September 22, 1962.

133   "It really makes you": Bill Shipp, "Assailant of FBI Man Put in Jail," *Atlanta Constitution*, September 10, 1962.

134   "There is little doubt": Martin Luther King Jr., "The Measure of a Man," *New York Amsterdam News*, September 29, 1962.

TWENTY: Backing the Birmingham Students

136   "Ain't gonna let segregation": For information about the history of the song, see Azizi Powell, ed., "Civil Rights Songs: Ain't Gonna Let Nobody Turn Me Around (lyrics & video)," Civilrightssongs.blogpost.com, November 29, 2014, civilrightssongs.blogspot.com/2014/11/aint-gonna-let-nobody-turn-me-around.html.

137   A dog named "Nigger": Cynthia Levinson, *We've Got a Job: The 1963 Birmingham Children's March* (Atlanta: Peachtree, 2012), 85.

138   "The revolution that is taking place": Jackie Robinson, telegram to John F. Kennedy, May 7, 1963, JRP, box 5, folder 14. See also Michael G. Long, ed., *First Class Citizenship: The Civil Rights Letters of Jackie Robinson* (New York: Times Books, 2007), 169.

138   "I don't like to be bitten" and "I don't like to,": "Jackie Robinson Plans to Join Birmingham Marchers," *Chicago Defender*, May 8, 1963.

139   "You can love them": "Troops on Alert in Birmingham," *Afro-American*, May 25, 1963.

140   "I don't think you realize": Taylor Branch, *Parting the Waters: America in the King Years* (New York: Simon and Schuster, 1988), 801.

140   "All those of you" and "Mr. Robinson": James L. Hicks, "Birmingham Sidelights," *New York Amsterdam News*, June 1, 1963.

140   "Don't worry about any bombs" and "Lightning never": James L. Hicks, "Jackie, Floyd Cause Happy Pandemonium in Birmingham," *New York Amsterdam News*, May 18, 1963.

TWENTY-ONE: Marching on Washington

142 "jam session": "*Life* Goes to Jackie Robinson's Jam Session," *Life*, July 5, 1963, p. 79.

142 "I can't understand": "Malcolm Inspires Egg Throwing and Booing in Harlem," *Atlanta Daily World*, July 3, 1963.

142 "go up there to Salem Church": "Malcolm Inspires Egg Throwing," July 3, 1963.

144 "for helping to create," "Malcolm has just," and "Malcolm X and his organization": Jackie Robinson, Home Plate, *New York Amsterdam News*, July 13, 1963.

144 "Will the police use" and "Are we going to jail?": Sharon Robinson, *Child of the Dream* (New York: Scholastic, 2019), 189.

144 "This is not Birmingham": Robinson, *Child of the Dream*, 190.

145 "I know all of us": "No Disorder as 110,000 Gather in Washington," Associated Press, August 28, 1963; see also Frank C. Giradot and Susan Abram, "Baseball Great Jackie Robinson Joined MLK at March on Washington," *Pasadena Star-News*, August 24, 2013.

145 WE MARCH FOR: The sign messages are drawn from photographs of the march, especially the lead photograph at NPR Staff, "'A People's History' of the March on Washington," *All Things Considered*, npr.org, August 2, 2010, npr.org/templates/story/story.php?storyId=129470920.

147 "I have a dream": Martin Luther King, Jr., "I Have a Dream," address delivered at the March on Washington for Jobs and Freedom, August 28, 1963, The Martin Luther King, Jr. Research and Education Institute, kinginstitutestanford.edu, no date, kinginstitute.stanford.edu /encyclopedia/i-have-dream.

147 "I have never been," "One had to be deeply moved," "What a beautiful," and "I am not so certain": Jackie Robinson, Home Plate, *New York Amsterdam News*, September 7, 1963.

TWENTY-TWO: Warring with Malcolm X

149 "If I had been a parent" and "God bless": Jackie Robinson, Home Plate, *New York Amsterdam News*, September 28, 1963.

150 "Yes, I'll be happy": Chuck Stone, "Defender Launches Drive for Ala. Church," *Chicago Defender*, September 17, 1963.

150   "the White Man": This phrase and other quotations from the letter come from "Malcolm X's Letter," *New York Amsterdam News*, November 30, 1963.

150   "Coming from you": This phrase and other quotations from the letter come from Jack Robinson, letter to Malcolm X, December 14, 1963, JRP, box 4, folder 35.

151   "White people will be shocked," "It is criminal," and "In areas where": M. S. Handler, "Malcolm X Sees Rise in Violence," *The New York Times*, March 13, 1964.

152   "We would really be," "What does this man," and "What is he really": Jackie Robinson, Home Plate, *New York Amsterdam News*, July 18, 1964.

153   "But I have always," and "The crack of those bullets": Jackie Robinson, "Crack of Bullets That Killed Malcolm X Will Have Echoes," *Philadelphia Tribune*, March 2, 1965.

153   "our ballot and our dollars": Jackie Robinson, Home Plate, *New York Amsterdam News*, October 22, 1966.

TWENTY-THREE: Crashing the White Man's Party

155   Jack called Goldwater "a bigot" and "an advocate of white supremacy": Jackie Robinson, Home Plate, July 4, 1964.

155   "a white man's party": Jackie Robinson, "The GOP: For White Men Only?" *The Saturday Evening Post* (August 10–17, 1963): 10.

156   WILL THE GOP BETRAY LINCOLN?: Ben Williams, "35,000 in Market St. Rights March," *San Francisco Examiner*, July 13, 1964.

156   GOLDWATER IS A RAT FINK and THE GRAND IMPERIAL WIZARDS: "Anti-Barry Rally Held by 35,000," *San Francisco Independent*, July 13, 1964.

156   "a bigot who will prevent us": "50,000 March 'No Goldwater,'" *Chicago Defender*, July 13, 1964.

156   there would be a "bloodbath": Rosemarie Tyler Books, "Negro GOP Delegates 100% Against Barry," *Chicago Defender*, July 13, 1964.

158   "C'mon Rocky!," "Turn him loose," and "I was ready": Robinson and Duckett, *I Never Had It Made*, 170.

159   "It is the only bank": Jackie Robinson, Home Plate, *New York Amsterdam News*, January 2, 1965.

TWENTY-FOUR: Defending Peace and War

163 "Go back to Africa": "Nazi Disrupts NAACP Dinner in Washington," *Minneapolis Star Tribune*, June 26, 1964.

163 "sending all the niggers," "Not only was my anger," and "They didn't hit him": All sentences from Robinson's explanation come from Jackie Robinson, Home Plate, July 11, 1964. For more on this incident, see "Jackie Robinson, Youths Boot Nazi from Banquet," *New Journal and Guide*, July 4, 1964.

163 "I will be very honest": Robinson, Home Plate, July 11, 1964.

164 "We're very fortunate," "We feel deeply," and "very wrong": "Robinson Speaks Up for Veterans in Viet Nam," *New Journal and Guide*, December 11, 1965.

164 "people with anti-war beliefs": Jackie Robinson, "Foes of Vietnam Policy Should Pause to Fight Dixie Murderers," *Philadelphia Tribune*, December 28, 1965.

165 King with being "unfair": Jackie Robinson, Home Plate, *New York Amsterdam News*, May 13, 1967.

165 "Before the rich," "brilliant," and "He is still": Jackie Robinson, Home Plate, July 1, 1967.

166 "You want me to do": See Howard Bingham and Max Wallace, *Muhammad Ali's Greatest Fight: Cassius Clay vs. The United States of America* (Lanham, MD: M. Evans, 2000), 149–50.

167 "In my view," "While I cannot," and "He was willing": All sentences from Robinson's response to Ali come from Jackie Robinson, Home Plate, *New York Amsterdam News*, October 14, 1967.

167 "I am convinced": Jackie Robinson, Home Plate, *New York Amsterdam News*, October 21, 1967.

TWENTY-FIVE: Refusing to Fly the Flag

169 "the greatest leader": Jackie Robinson, Home Plate, *New York Amsterdam News*, April 13, 1968.

169 "He has a right" and "No one ever": Jackie Robinson, Home Plate, *New York Amsterdam News*, March 23, 1968.

170 "The Republican Party": Jackie Robinson, Home Plate, *New York Amsterdam News*, August 17, 1968.

172   "Improper reporting": "Panther Aim Is Defended by Robinson," *Daily News* (New York), September 13, 1968.

172   "The Black Panthers seek": "Robinson Backs Defense of Black Group, but Mrs. Basie Defers," *Muhammad Speaks*, October 4, 1968.

172   "They [the Panthers] had every reason": "Panther Aim Is Defended by Robinson," September 13, 1968.

172   "trigger-happy": "Robinson Backs Defense of Black Group, but Mrs. Basie Defers," October 4, 1968.

172   "law and order": For Robinson's reaction to the phrase with regard to the Black Panthers, see Jackie Robinson, Home Plate, September 22, 1968.

172   "If we expect Law and Order": Jackie Robinson, letter to the editor, *New York Amsterdam News*, April 12, 1969.

173   "I wouldn't fly the flag" and "captive": Jon Nordheimer, "Flag on July 4: Thrill to Some, Threat to Others," *The New York Times*, July 4, 1969.

173   "I cannot stand": Robinson and Duckett, *I Never Had It Made*, xxiv.

173   "dangerous confrontation," "On my way," and "Thinking over that incident": Robinson and Duckett, *I Never Had It Made*, 272.

TWENTY-SIX: Heading Home

175   "I had gone weak" and "I knew": Robinson and Duckett, *I Never Had It Made*, 246.

176   "This is truly": Rampersad, *Jackie Robinson*, 456.

177   "I am grieved": "Ex-Dodger Builds Apartments," *Afro-American*, September 23, 1972.

177   "I am extremely proud": A video of this event is available at "Jackie Robinson Gives Final Speech at 1972 World Series," https://www.youtube.com/watch?v=Pdg0WApbYjI&t=22s.

178   "So I ran out": *Jackie Robinson*, episode 2, directed by Ken Burns, Sarah Burns, and David McMahon, produced by Florentine Films and WETA in Washington, DC, in association with Major League Baseball, 2016.

179   "When Jackie took the field": "Jackie Robinson Steals Home," *New York Amsterdam News*, October 28, 1972.

180 "A life is not important": A photograph of the inscribed tombstone is at Lore Croghan, "Jackie Robinson, Mae West and Piet Mondrian Rest in Peace at Cypress Hills Cemetery," Brooklyneagle.com, April 5, 2017, brooklyneagle.com/articles/2017/04/05/jackie-robinson-mae-west-and -piet-mondrian-rest-in-peace-at-cypress-hills-cemetery.

IMAGE CREDITS

Grateful acknowledgment to the following for the use of the images in this book:

ii Hulton Archive, Getty Images / 5 Georgia Historical Society / 6 Library of Congress, Getty Images / 8 Georgia Archives, Vanishing Georgia Collection / 9 Georgia Archives, Vanishing Georgia Collection / 10 Hulton Archive, Getty Images / 12 Schomburg Center for Research in Black Culture, Jean Blackwell Hutson Research and Reference Division, New York Public Library / 15 Hulton Archive, Getty Images / 16 Southern California News Group / 17 Southern California News Group / 19 Southern California News Group / 21 Southern California News Group / 24 Pasadena Public Library, Pasadena, California / 25 Pasadena Public Library, Pasadena, California / 28 Library of Congress / 29 Pasadena Public Library, Pasadena, California / 33 *The Sequoian* yearbook, 1935, courtesy of John Muir High School Alumni Association / 35 Southern California News Group / 36 *The Sequoian* yearbook, 1935, courtesy of John Muir High School Alumni Association / 37 *The Sequoian* yearbook, 1937, courtesy of John Muir High School Alumni Association / 38 Pasadena City College yearbook, 1939, Pasadena City College Library, Pasadena, California / 40 Southern California News Group / 41 (all) Pasadena City College yearbook, 1939, Pasadena City College Library, Pasadena, California / 43 *Chicago Defender* / 46 Library of Congress, Getty Images / 50 Southern California News Group / 51 (top) Southern California News Group; (bottom) Bettmann, Getty Images / 53 (clockwise from upper left) UCLA Library Special Collections; AP Photo; UCLA Library Special Collections; AP Photo / 57 Archive Photos, Getty Images / 60 African American Museum & Library at Oakland, Oakland Public Library / 61 Southern California News Group /

62 *Chicago Defender* / 63 Archive Photos, Getty Images / 64 National Archives / 67 National Archives / 70 Bettmann, Getty Images / 72 Heritage Images, Getty Images / 74 Transcendental Graphics, Getty Images / 76 AFRO-American Newspapers / 78 Sports Studio Photos, Getty Images / 79 FPG, Getty Images / 83 AP Photo, John Lent / 85 Bettmann, Getty Images / 86 AFRO-American Newspapers / 88 Photographs and Prints Division, Schomburg Center for Research in Black Culture, New York Public Library / 90 Irving Haberman, H Images, Getty Images / 92 C. M. Battey, Getty Images / 93 *Elizabethton Star* / 98 (from left) California African American Museum, Collection of the California African American Museum, gift of Eleanor Mead Schlinger, in memory of her father, Rufus Mead, Principal of Muir Technical High School; Lelands; Heritage Auctions, HA.com / 99 AFRO-American Newspapers / 100 Bettmann, Getty Images / 101 *New Journal and Guide*, Norfolk, Virginia / 102 *Pittsburgh Courier* Archives / 103 AFP, Getty Images / 106 AP Photo, William J. Smith / 110 AFRO-American Newspapers / 113 AP Photo, Gene Smith / 117 (both) Frank Hurley, New York *Daily News* Archive, Getty Images / 123 AFRO Newspaper, Gado, Getty Images / 124 Teenie Harris Archive, Carnegie Museum of Art, Getty Images / 126 AP Photo, Jack Harris / 128 Department of the Interior, National Park Service, National Capital Parks, National Archives / 130 Bettmann, Getty Images / 132 National Baseball Hall of Fame Library, Getty Images / 135 Frank Rockstroh, Michael Ochs Archives, Getty Images / 136 AFRO Newspaper, Gado, Getty Images / 139 Bettman, Getty Images / 141 AP Photo / 143 Fred W. McDarrah, Getty Images / 146 Steve Schapiro, Getty Images / 148 Birmingham, Alabama, Public Library Archives / 151 AFRO-American Newspapers / 154 *New Journal and Guide*, Norfolk, Virginia / 156 Bettmann, Getty Images / 157 Library of Congress, Prints & Photographs Division, © David S. Johnson / 165 New York *Daily News* Archive, Getty Images / 166 AP Photo / 168 © Constantine Manos, Magnum Photos / 175 Bettmann, Getty Images / 178 Bettmann, Getty Images / 179 AFRO-American Newspapers / 180 Bettmann, Getty Images

INDEX